DO YOU LOVE ME
MORE THAN THESE?

DO YOU LOVE ME MORE THAN THESE?

Lord, why are You asking this question?

WILLIAM LINN RUTHERFORD

XULON PRESS

Xulon Press
2301 Lucien Way #415
Maitland, FL 32751
407.339.4217
www.xulonpress.com

© 2021 by William Linn Rutherford

Unless otherwise indicated, Scripture quotations taken from the Revised Standard Version (RSV). Copyright © 1946, 1952, and 1971 the Division of Christian Education of the National Council of the Churches of Christ in the United States of America. Used by permission. All rights reserved.

Paperback ISBN-13: 978-1-6628-2947-5
eBook ISBN-13: 978-1-6628-2948-2

Acknowledgement

The pastor's hair was graying, yet his countenance seemed far more vibrant than his age. In his arms, close to his heart, he cradled a child who was only months old. The parents watched with delight as he tenderly spoke with her and smiled into her eyes, and received a smile back. He slowly walked among the congregation so everyone could see the precious child from God he was blessed to be holding, and to bless in Jesus' name.

The pastor embodied such genuine affection, familiarity, and joy for the little one it was as if he was related to her and to the family. More than fifty years have passed since his smile shone upon that child's face; still, the gentleness and effect of the Spirit of God in and through him remains vivid in my mind.

Since then, I have recognized the presence of God's Spirit in countless people who have reached out to someone, in some way, with the same peacefulness, comfort and love I witnessed that day.

No special occasion is required to manifest the presence of the Holy Spirit in us. The acts of selflessness we share with one another bear witness to His presence. The care and compassion we have for one another confirms His presence. The forgiveness and restoration we extend to one another demonstrates His presence. Our desire to apply His Spirit in all we do for the glory of Jesus verifies His presence.

I have reflected often on the wonderful heart and the genuine joy I observed as the pastor held the child in his arms, but I no longer wonder if they were related. Now I know they were.

God's Spirit was present and powerful in the pastor, blessing him to see as God sees, to love as God loves, to hold the precious child close to his heart, as God does.

We, too, are blessed by the power of the Holy Spirit to be related to one another in the same way; seeing with His eyes, loving with His love, cradling with His arms, and reflecting His tender smile. Thank You, Holy Spirit, for Your presence; for Your power; for Your passion and for Your love in us, through us, and for us.

William Linn Rutherford

Preface

To love someone with all of our heart and with all of our devotion is an act of our will. It is not something that another forces upon us, persuades us of, or that we surrender too unwillingly. Many things may influence us, including those who would manipulate us, but our will is not determined for us; it is determined by us.

We love because we choose to love. We give our heart because we choose to give it. We are faithful because we choose to be faithful. Our passion, spirit, words, actions, and thoughts are what we choose. They are an outward expression of an inward condition. Each one is our decision—each one is evidence of our will.

Invariably, our will identifies us with someone or something. How could it not? If we are devoted to them, agree with them, align with them, rejoice with them, suffer with them and seek to honor them, we will be identified with them. We may even become more like them because of all we have in common with them.

How much thought do we give to why we choose to love and to whom we choose to give our heart? Some have written exacting specifications describing what they are looking for, others may utilize computer apps to introduce and match them with another, and some still meet the old-fashioned way, by chance. Yet it is not by chance that we give our love to someone—it is by our will.

Table of Contents

CHAPTER I

The Question

"Simon, son of John, do you love me more than these?"
"Yes, Lord; you know that I love you" (John 21:15).

Again Jesus asked, *"Simon son of John, do you love me?"* Peter answered, *"Yes, Lord; you know that I love you."* A third time Jesus said, *"Simon, son of John, do you love me?"* Simon Peter responded, *"Lord, you know everything; you know that I love you."*

This brief conversation was witnessed by several people. Any confusion the onlookers may have had about what our Lord was asking and how Peter was answering must have been resolved by the time they heard the question and the reply for the third time. We have been blessed to hear it, too.

Why did Jesus ask such an important, personal question with a group listening to the conversation? Was it because Peter had denied Jesus with a group listening to what he said? Was it so Peter could learn that nothing he said or did or thought was hidden from Jesus? Was it to make known that Peter's boastful pride, and then his fearfulness, was not from God? Was it so Peter could discover and confess his true heart for the Lord?

Was it to make public the great privilege and sacred steward-ship Jesus was entrusting to Peter? Or, was it as much for those who were listening, and for us, as it was for Peter?

It certainly gave everyone time to consider how they would respond if Jesus were to ask them the question. It gives us the same opportunity. Are we ready to reply?

One way to find out is to replace Peter's name with our own and answer the question with others listening to our response: "_____, son of _____, do you love me more than these?"

- "Ahhh, more than what, Lord?"
- "Do I have to answer right now?"
- "Why does it matter who I love most?"
- "Does my answer have to be *yes* or *no*?"
- "How can I respond without offending someone?"
- "Aren't we supposed to love everyone without partiality?"
- "Can we please discuss this another time, in private?"
- "Lord, you know everything. Why are you asking me the question?"

We may understand why the question was asked if we con-sider times we have asked someone a question to which we already knew the answer. Assuming our motive was to help them, which can surely be said of Jesus, then their response was not primarily for our benefit, but for theirs, and perhaps for someone who was listening to the conversation.

Consider Peter's spirit when he heard the question. Earlier, he had said in a group setting that he would never deny the Lord; yet he did, publicly, repeatedly and vehemently. He also said that he would never forsake the Lord; but he did, publicly, cowardly and sorrowfully. Peter's pride and self-confidence did not help him when fear gripped his heart. He did the very thing he thought he would never do; he denied and abandoned the Lord.

He was ashamed of himself. He lost his way. He went from strength to weakness, from faithfulness to denial, from self-assurance to self-contempt, from fellowship to fear. And there were witnesses to all of it.

Yet the Lord's boundless grace restored Peter and the question helped Peter regain focus on what mattered to him most. Not even his great pride could keep Peter from confessing in the presence of others, *"Yes Lord, I love you."* Peter was freed from the burden he had inflicted and carried upon himself by the power, peace and love of Christ Jesus.

Though Peter had earlier testified that Jesus was *"the Christ, the Son of the Living God"* (Matthew 3:16), he did not proclaim his love for the Lord until he was asked the question. Perhaps the question was a surprise to Peter, something he never expected would be asked of him. When we are asked something completely unexpected, we may not know what to say or whether to speak at all, especially with others listening. Yet Peter did not hesitate to answer, and he did not answer the question with a question. He said, *"Yes Lord; you know that I love you."* He was right; Jesus did know. Peter's answer was not for the Lord's sake. It was for Peter's sake and for the sake of those who were listening, then and now.

With his answer, Peter expressed his true heart for the Lord. How could Peter not have known his own heart previously? Maybe he was consumed by his work, or focused on all of the people with whom he was interacting or impressed by his expanding influence and prestige. If that were so, his mind may have been on things other than Jesus, like himself. Being "full of ourselves" can happen to anyone. When it does, we can forget who we are working for and what is most important to them.

Peter's schedule may have been busy; filled with meetings, activities, travel, challenges, endless hours and great opportunities. His walk with Jesus was a big change for the former fisherman. With big changes our expectations, desires and priorities experience big changes, too.

This is one reason Peter's reply to the question was so memorable. Peter was a self-made man, or so he thought, as many of us do. He followed his own path, set his own agenda and worked the way he determined was best. His arduous occupation may have made his physical stature formidable. His habit of self-aggrandizement could have conveyed by word or deed that he did not need anyone. It is unlikely a man with Peter's life experience, perspective and work habits would voluntarily submit to anyone, let alone serve them and make their purpose, their words, and their ways his own.

With that in mind, those who heard Peter's answer must have been startled by the change in him. His strength and standing were no longer in himself; they were in Jesus. With each answer he gave to the Lord's question, Jesus gave Peter direction, privilege and trust.

- *'Do you love more than these?' 'Yes Lord!' "Feed my lambs."*
- *'Do you love me?' 'Yes Lord!' "Tend my sheep."*
- *'Do you love me?' 'Yes Lord!' "Feed my sheep."*

Jesus entrusted the stewardship of His beloved Church, which had not even been established yet, to the one who thought he had committed the unforgiveable sin; who had not kept his word; who sank under the weight of his own brokenness and failure.

When we fail to stand with Jesus as we thought we would; and when we deny Him at school, work, the ballot box or some other public place as we never thought we could; and when we make ourselves or someone else more important than Him; that is the time to remember when Jesus addressed the question to Peter. It was in the midst of heartache. It was after Peter had tried to see what would happen to the Lord, but did not want to be seen as a follower of the Lord. It was when Peter was looking for the Lord's salvation, but seeing His suffering. It was when Peter's hopes were dying. These are times our faith is tested; not for God's edification, but for our own. It may be when we discover who is really for us, who will get on their knees with us; whose grace, mercy, and love saves us, and who matters most to us.

When we are conformed to the world more than we are to Jesus, it shows in our decisions and actions. It may be the moment the Lord asks the question of us: *"Do you love me more than these?"*

Each of us will reply, if not with words then by the motive in our heart, by the choices we make, by those with whom we align ourselves, by the principles we hold onto and what we let go; and by what we plant, cultivate and grow with our words, spirit and deeds. Our answer, like Peter's, may be as much for those with whom we interact as it is for us. Jesus already knows.

Why Must We Answer the Question?

Keep in mind what the prophet Jeremiah said: the human heart is *"deceitful and corrupt above all things"* (Jeremiah 17:9). Peter is not the only one who says one thing and does another. He is not the only one who holds himself in high regard. He is not the only one whose pride rules his mind. He is not the only one who chooses himself over the one he serves. He is not the only one who denies and abandons the Lord. He is not the only one whose shame and guilt wears on his mind. He is not the only one who runs away. He is not the only one who believes separation from God is what he wants or deserves. However, this is not what Jesus thought or what He ordained when He said to Peter, *"Follow me!"* (John 21:22).

Peter needed to answer the question, not only to understand his own heart, but to receive his stewardship. Jesus knew His plan for Peter and the blessings that would accompany it, but Peter needed to know what mattered most to him. Only then could he apply and share what Christ had prepared for him from before the foundation of the world.

The same applies to us. We cannot receive what we do not believe. We cannot share what we have not been given. We cannot honor what we do not defend. Our answer, like Peter's, reveals the one who is our source, sustainer, purpose and fulfillment.

- This is the one for whom we live.
- This person is our foundation, hope and help.
- This person inspires our thoughts, words and actions.
- This person is the lens through which we see the world.
- This person is the one we identify with and in whom we rejoice.
- This person is the light to our path and to our destination.
- This person is who we rely upon and trust above all.
- This person is our greatest comfort and defense.
- This person is our heartbeat, home and peace.
- This person loves us even when others ignore us.
- This person is the one we serve and lift up.
- This person is our strength and salvation.
- This person is where we want to be.
- This person is who we need.

We may choose different words to describe what this person means to us, but our descriptions will have this much in common—this person is the one who matters most to us.

Perhaps it is our spouse or child who means the most to us, but they are not our source. Maybe we identify with our social network or inner circle of friends and associates, but they are not the sustainer of our life. It may be a celebrity or a team we identify with, but they are not the purpose of our life. Or, maybe the one we love best and lift-up most is ourselves, but we are not the reason we live.

There is only one who is our source, sustainer, purpose and completion: our beginning and end. In this context, our answer to the question says as much about us as it does the one we love.

What we say and do impacts them, which is why what matters to them matters to us.

Jesus said, *"If you love me, you will keep my commandments"* (John 14:15). Because this matters to Jesus, it matters to us. We can receive God's Word and direction and keep it, or we can receive someone else's. Our spirit reveals the choice we have made.

- We do not love God by ignoring His Word.
- We do not love God by disobeying His Word.
- We do not love God by changing His Word.
- We do not love God by failing to pray in His Spirit.
- We do not love God by refusing to forgive.
- We do not love God by hurting one another.
- We do not love God by attributing to happenstance His creation.
- We do not love God by unfaithfulness to Him.
- We do not love God by justifying and celebrating our sins.
- We do not love God by denying Him our praise and service.
- We do not love God by valuing someone's approval above His.
- We do not love God by forgetting His cross, His blood, His death, His burial, His resurrection, and His return.
- We do not love God if we keep His saving grace to ourselves

Love for God is lived by protecting, serving and lifting up what He has entrusted to our care; for it all belongs to Him.

We may forget this or choose not to believe it. After all, no one did the work for us. No one studied for us or took the tests for us. No one lifted the weights for us or competed in the game for us. No one suffered injuries for us or bore the burden for us. No one crossed the finish line for us — at least not that we noticed.

God's providence, protection and purpose, in and through it all, may be overlooked or rejected. Yet, our capacity to study and learn, our health and strength and our ability to persevere and succeed are all from Him. We can believe otherwise and say that our achievement is a result of our work, dedication, strategy and team, but with that point of view we miss one of life's greatest opportunities: to join our voice with all of Heaven's in giving glory and thanks to God. The glory we give Him, unlike credit we claim for ourselves and each other, never fades and is never forgotten.

We also miss the fleeting moment to speak with someone who is listening to what we say. They may have no idea of the mighty work God has done, or the tremendous inheritance He has given to us that so many others have faithfully protected and provided for us. Perhaps one of the reasons the capacity and moment to achieve is temporarily in our care is simply this: to speak and to glorify God.

Our words and actions reveal whether we are keeping His commandments or not. Our remorse and repentance when we fail to do so confirm our love for Him is real. The way we respond to His discipline and blessings reveal our reliance on Him and our relationship with Him.

Reflecting on who supports us, guides us, and walks with us depends on how well we truly know them. This requires giving them our time and attention, listening to what they say, watching what they do, learning from them, following them, experiencing their kindness, committing our heart to them and discovering that their heart was committed to us long before we knew.

Evidence of their spirit in us is shown by the choices we make, by what we approve and defend, by the tone of our words, by the motive of our heart and the product of our lives.

There are times we choose distance from them or even rush off in another direction losing sight of them completely, like a great dog chasing after a compelling scent through the woods, only to discover what he sought was not that great and his master is not where he left him. Now he runs to catch up and finds his master waiting and looking for him. Overjoyed to be together again, they return to their walk.

The One We Walk With

Who we walk with, the direction we go, the rabbit trails we chase, and our faithfulness to them shows up in the steps we take. But paying attention to our daily steps can be difficult, even when walking with our best friend. There are so many appealing people and places that capture our interest, consume our time and draw us away. There are so many burdens and strife, in and around us, which can separate us from one another and keep us apart.

Yet no matter how far off-course we go from the direction we were heading, it may seem that our path is just fine (perhaps even better) and it really does not matter because it all leads to the same destination, eventually.

That would be like setting out on a walk through a vast and unfamiliar forest, confident that whatever direction we take is safe and will lead us home. Then, as the sun begins to set, after countless steps through brush and woods, we discover we are nowhere near where we thought we would be — not even close. Worse, those who trusted and walked with us are lost, too.

It would be an immense help to know someone who lives where we want to go; who has made the trip before us; who is able and willing to guide us, and who we choose to follow. By their side, encouraged by their wisdom and strength, we walk through valleys, climb rocky slopes and traverse high ridges. At vantage points along the way, we catch glimpses of our destination (assurance that we are going the right way). We also see paths that are wide and well worn, that many have followed, but not our guide.

The Paths

These vantage points present temptations that test how much we trust our guide and reveal our heart for the way he is leading. The wide path is more travelled than the narrow one. The guide who leads us on the narrow path is not the guide who leads on the wide path. Differences in the paths reflect the differences in the guides. We cannot be on the wide way and profess to follow the guide who leads on the narrow way. Nor can we be on the narrow path and profess to follow the guide who leads on the wide way. The way of our heart and the way of our guide are one in the same. This must be so or we are not being true to ourselves or to our guide, for our guide knows whether we follow his leading. Remember, Jesus said, "*If you love me you will keep my commandments.*" Our response to other paths indicates the presence or absence of our faith and trust in our guide.

In our daily routine, and during times of difficulty, our faith in the path and in our guide either grows or declines; but it does not stay the same. We have confidence in our guide and his leading, or our confidence is in someone or something else. It depends on who and what we believe and the choices we make. If we truly believe the one in whom we place our faith and know that he is in control, then our faith grows stronger by applying it and draws us closer to our guide. It is "*through faith for faith*" (Romans 1:17) that our faith becomes more than when we first believed.

Gifts Given and Received

A picture of this wonderful Scripture can be seen in the seeds of God's trees. Their embryo contains a root, stem, and leaves. Upon sprouting, the tiny tree does not receive more root, stem or leaves. These grow through their use and in response to God's grace of air, soil, water and light. As more leaves grow, more light is received. As roots grow, more moisture is received. As wood grows, more strength and capacity is received. Applying the gifts of God and receiving the grace of God, trees become more than they were when they first began to grow.

However, trees of the same species with the same conditions of air, soil, water and light do not necessarily grow to maturity the same way. Why not? If their access to God's grace is the same and their exposure to risks are the same, something about their condition, their interactions with each other and/or their surroundings must account for differences in their growth.

Perhaps the reason is low vitality and weak resistance to what can harm them. Perhaps wounds from past injuries have not been compartmentalized, which compromises their capacity to cope with new attacks. Perhaps stress progresses to strain, disrupting or separating connections upon which they depend. Perhaps a variety of agents act in concert with one another to the detriment of their growth and well-being.

Growth, however, is not optional. In the absence of growth, trees exhaust their resources and their health declines. Trees live to grow and they grow to live. This requires utilizing their root system, stem and foliage where they are planted. Applying their gifts and receiving the provisions they are supplied enables them to grow.

Like embryonic trees, our faith must be used in order to grow. With the growth, more grace is poured in, which produces more faith. Without growth, however, the capacity of faith is unchanged. More cannot be poured into a container that does not use what it has, nor can more be added to the vessel if it is full of something else. Yet, trees and faith do receive more when they use what they have to the glory of God. One expresses it by ascending in praise, the other by bowing in humility — both exalt God.

For this reason, if our answer to the question is, *"Yes, Lord, you know that I love you,"* we want to be baptized for the glory of God. Doing so testifies that Jesus is our Lord. Like the marriage ceremony affirms love for our spouse, baptism affirms love for

Jesus. In each case, the life-changing oneness we share with them is celebrated with our family and friends, as is our joy about being united and identified with them.

Marriage and Baptism

Marriage and baptism share another connection. Each is devoted to the one we live for and the one who lives for us. Where there is love, there is marriage. Where there is love, there is baptism.

Baptism, like marriage, is a voluntary act of our will. We marry because we love and want to publicly acknowledge our commitment to our spouse. We are baptized because we love and want to publicly identify with the life, death, burial and resurrection of our Savior.

Before our Lord ascended into Heaven, He said, *"baptize them in the name of the Father, the Son and of the Holy Spirit"* (Matthew 28:19). Jesus was speaking about all who would believe in Him and follow Him. No one else can make the decision for us or be baptized for us. For example, infant baptism represents the heart of the parents, not the child. We cannot choose to be baptized, whether a child or an adult, without understanding who Jesus is and what He has done for us; confessing Him as Lord of our life and willingly, joyfully, and publicly identifying ourselves with Him.

Salvation comes by grace through faith in Jesus (see Ephesians 2:8). Without believing Jesus is Lord, baptism is void of the meaning of His suffering, death and resurrection, which we share through baptism. The Holy Spirit convicts us of our sins, brings us to our Savior, and inspires us to be baptized; but it is our spirit that chooses to be immersed in the water and raised to new life in Him.

The sacrament affirms we are Jesus' and He is ours. It is love reflecting love. It ascends and bows before the throne of God to the glory of God.

Loving God and glorifying God are wonderful states of heart, but they are not the same. Consider all of the people we love. There are many, but our love is not the same for each one. In fact, there may be little or no communication with some of them; yet there is love. However, it is not love that glorifies; it is not love that sustains. Love can exist without glorification, but glorification cannot occur without love.

Glorifying Jesus begins with loving Jesus. *"Do you love me more than these?"* acknowledges there is love for Jesus. It also acknowledges there is a hierarchy of love within each of us. This ranking exists, no matter how much we may object or deny that we love one person more or differently than another. Our Lord would not have asked the question if we loved everyone the same.

So, there is a ranking of our own making. Even if we have never spoken their name out loud, someone is in that place of honor in each of our lives. The decisions we make and the spirit we share in our conversations and interactions with others provides evidence of who holds this place of honor. Does the evidence point to honoring Jesus or to someone, or something, else? If we say we don't know, we are not being honest. Either we do not want to answer the question, or we do not want others to know our answer.

We seldom struggle to share our love for a celebrity, a friend or a beloved pet. However, ease of expressing words and sharing deeds of love for our Creator, Sustainer and Savior is not so readily extended. Why does it matter? After all, Jesus knows.

It matters, in part, for reasons similar to why we often, and with strong conviction, talk about our connection with a friend, a lifestyle or a political point of view. We want people to know how we feel, and why. We talk about what matters to us; our priority and passion.

It matters for a more important reason. Jesus said, *"Everyone who acknowledges me before men, I will also acknowledge before my Father who is in Heaven; but whoever denies me before men, I also will deny before my Father who is in Heaven"* (Matthew 10:32-33).

How can that be? Jesus forgave Peter, who denied Him publicly, and Jesus died for us before we even knew or loved Him. That is true, but Peter's heart was grieved by his denial of Jesus. Are we grieved when we deny Him? A symptom of great love is great grief when separated from the one we love.

Based on Peter's denial of the Lord, it is clear that Jesus does not deny us before the Father due to our weakness in a crisis or an inflated perspective of ourselves. If that were so, many of us could end up being denied. That is not the case, however, for Jesus knows who loves Him and He knows if our grief is an expression of our love for Him, or simply an indication of regret.

Where there is little recognition of this, there is also little love for Jesus. Like the Pharisee who did not perceive his own desperate need loved Jesus only a little. In contrast, the woman who washed Jesus' feet with her tears and dried them with her hair recognized her need and loved Jesus much. One acknowledged Jesus as Lord, the other did not. What we perceive is what we tend to acknowledge.

When the Pharisee condemned the woman and judged the Lord, the Pharisee made his rejection of them clear. *"If this man were a prophet, he would have known who and what sort of woman this is who is touching him, for she is a sinner"* (Luke 7:39). The Pharisee's mind was made up. Nothing anyone said, nor the mighty works Jesus did, would change his mind or heart. He did not believe Jesus was omniscient. He did not believe Jesus was doing the work of God. He did not believe Jesus was God. He did not perceive his own sinfulness.

Not believing our own sinfulness and our need for Jesus to save us is the bedrock of rejecting Him.

Lifelong refusal to see and repent of our sins is basis enough for denial before God. Ignoring or scorning Jesus' love for us and the death He died for us is, too. Why would we acknowledge the great price He paid if we do not recognize the great debt we owe? After all, we cannot love Jesus most if we do not need Jesus most.

From childhood to old age we are drawn to our heart's desire—to what we believe, to who we love, and to what we want. We do not esteem or honor that which we are not drawn to or desire. We do not walk with Jesus unless we choose to.

Trusting and following Jesus comes from being rooted in His love by the work of the Holy Spirit in us. If we have Jesus, we have the Holy Spirit. Then we are drawn to Jesus, we value and want more of Him; we believe and love Him and we acknowledge Him before our family, friends and those God blesses us to know. Saying His name and sharing His love is not a hardship or an embarrassment; it is a privilege and a blessing. In contrast, if we do not love Jesus, we do not talk about Him; we do not rejoice when someone else talks about Him; and we do not *"glorify His name above every name"* (Ephesians 1:21). The Holy Spirit makes Him known and inspires this in us.

That is why the question Jesus asked Peter (and us) is not just a warm-up question preceding something bigger or more important. There is nothing more important or bigger! What we decide about Jesus impacts everything we do, everything we are. If our answer is, *"Yes, Lord, you know that I love you"* we are no longer our own, we belong to the Lord and He belongs to us.

Consider how our views and priorities change when we love someone. We cherish their presence; we long to hear their voice; we want to be a blessing to them; we talk about them with joy and thanksgiving; we cannot bear the thought of them being hurt, neglected or rejected. Yet, we may go weeks, months or years without mentioning Jesus to anyone. God said, *"My people have forgotten me days without end"* (Jeremiah 2:32).

How can this be so if there is love? How it must please those who mock Jesus when we say nothing. How our silence must grieve the Spirit of God.

Perhaps we do not have opportunities to talk about Jesus; or if we do, we may not know what to say; or we may prefer others to speak for us about Jesus; or maybe we need more time to decide how to handle it. However, not making a decision is a decision.

We talk with affection and ease about our loved ones. No one needs to speak for us. We share a word, a picture or a story almost spontaneously; not because of the opportunity, but because of the love. There is no hesitation in our spirit or uncertainty in our thoughts. We talk about them because we love them.

Do our friends and acquaintances even care? Do they want to hear what we say? Does it make any difference to their lives? It may, it may not, but those are not the reasons that we share. We share not to change someone else's heart; we share because our heart is changed.

Love gives us meaning, identity and strength. It inspires our thoughts, words, decisions and deeds. It makes us better. We take the focus off ourselves. Love honors God and keeps His Word. "*For the love of Christ controls us, for we are convinced that one has died for all; therefore all have died. And He died for all, that those who live might no longer live for them-selves but for Him who for their sake died and was raised*" (2 Corinthians 5:14-15).

Love Changes Us

We may not consider it in these terms, but our love does inspire and control us. Whether it is love for our family, our work, a cause, or our Lord—what we do (and what we do not do) reflects who we love and to whom we belong. Some may call this conscience or morality, but more than that, it is love. It is not subjective or situational. It is not a feeling or a fantasy. It is absolute, unwavering and foundational. It is putting others ahead of ourselves. It is rejoicing when they rejoice and suffering when they suffer. It is seeing with their eyes, listening with their ears, speaking with their heart, serving with their spirit and making their goals our own.

The thought of doing this may be foreign or even undesirable to those of us who have our own self-centered plans and goals. How can we fulfill our desires if our focus is on fulfilling someone else's? If self-interest is our priority, then we may not be able to help someone fulfill their goals. Our answer to the question may be, "No, I do not love you more than these and I will not change." If our priority is Jesus, then our reply is, "Yes, I do love you more than these and what you want is what I want." Then our heart's desire is fulfilled because what we want is made new by the one we love.

What about the goals we had before we loved Christ? Do they remain? Are they achieved? Time will tell, but if they are not of God and for the glory of God, then where are they from, and whom do they please? Our goals and priorities are connected to the one we serve and love.

The Lord's question is pretty straight forward. Do our words, choices, deeds and thoughts bless and honor Christ Jesus, or not? We know if they do; and we know if they do not. We affirm our answer by acknowledging Jesus is Lord or by denying Him; by keeping His Word or by ignoring it; by loving Him or rejecting Him; by serving Him or refusing Him; by looking forward to His return or dreading it, by sharing His saving grace or by not speaking of it; by following where He leads or by following someone else; by knowing He is the source and Savior of life or by not believing it; and by trusting all that we do and all that we pray to His care; or by not having faith in Him.

What about the times we have trusted and called upon Jesus for help, but our prayers seemed not to be answered, at least not in the way we wanted? What about the strife, violence, division and suffering in the world? What about all the burdens and barriers in our lives? Where is Jesus in these?

He is as close as we want Him to be. He is as close as we let Him be. He is as close as we believe Him to be. He is as close as He said He would be, *"I am with you always"* (Matthew 28:20).

A better question is: Am I with Jesus? Am I following Him? Am I faithful to Him? Do I believe He is the Creator of earth, sea and sky and the Savior and Judge of us all? Do I love Him? If this answer is yes, then even in the midst of struggles and sorrows we remember that Jesus went through struggles and sorrows, too.

When we cry out to God for help, we remember Jesus did, too. There was nothing about His life that kept His prayers from being heard and answered by God, because He was not at odds with God. When we pray, we remember how Jesus prayed and what He did. He trusted God, saying, *"Not as I will, but as Thou wilt"* (Matthew 26:39). When this is our prayer, we rest in the knowledge, peace and grace of God, whose ways and thoughts are higher and better than ours. We know that in His Holy presence are eternal joy, blessings, and life.

Nevertheless, our love for family and friends may lead us to believe that nothing could be better than the here and now and the life we have together, even though we do not always act that way. There may be times when we treat one another as if we do not like each other; let alone love each other. The separation and unkindness that results may last a few hours or days or longer, but beneath it is hope for the future. However, hope that does not endure and trust is not grounded in the love of God. It cannot help us recover from heartbreak. It cannot strengthen us when we are without strength. It cannot save us. It cannot unite us. Without hope, there can be great distances between us and great distance from God.

Rooted In Jesus

When our hope is rooted in the love of Christ Jesus, our daily joys do not cease. Our spirit of gratitude for each new day and every person in our lives (past, present and future) does not wane. Despair does not prevail. God's presence in us overcomes the darkness around us. The love of Christ has no partnership with darkness. With Christ in us, we cannot stop singing, sharing and serving. We cannot stop giving Him praise. We cannot keep from being blessed by His Word. We cannot keep from praying in His Spirit. We cannot stop loving Him, even if we do not understand His Sovereign Will. *"For I am sure that neither death nor life, nor angels, nor principalities, nor things present, nor things to come, nor powers, nor height, nor depth, nor anything else in all creation, will be able to separate us from the love of God in Christ Jesus our Lord"* (Romans 8:38-39). Jesus is the source and object of our faith.

To give up hope and to withdraw from the joys and duties of life is to withdraw from Jesus, the author of life, the reason for life and the confidence of our hope today and our hope for tomorrow. There is a reason, *"The Lord takes pleasure in those who fear Him, in those who hope in His steadfast love"* (Psalm 147:11). These are people who stand with Him when they barely have strength to stand; who trust Him above all; and who call on Him with everlasting thanksgiving. Nevertheless, our reverence and reliance upon Jesus is not a free pass from suffering and sorrow. It is, however, a sure way through them and a testimony of our faith in it.

Faithfulness and submission to God are less difficult when all is well. It is when things are not well that we need more than what we have in ourselves, even more than what our loved ones and friends can share with us. We require the source of life, love, hope, faith, courage, strength and peace. Jesus is that source. He is grace in the midst of gracelessness; faith in the midst of unfaithfulness; hope in the midst of crisis; holy in the midst of ungodliness; life in the midst of loss; sovereign in the midst of suffering. He is fulfillment even when the answer to prayer is delayed or denied.

When the apostle Paul prayed for God to remove an afflic-tion he suffered, he prayed again and again, but was not cured. Though a venomous snake bit him and he was not harmed;

though he cast out a demon from a girl by speaking a word; though he restored life to a boy who had died, Paul could not help, or rid himself of his own affliction. God said, *"My grace is sufficient for you, for my power is made perfect in weakness"* (2 Corinthians 12:9). This mighty man of God did not have his prayer answered the way he wanted. For some of us, that may have been justification for bitterness, anger, disillusionment or leaving the faith.

Although Job was a man of extraordinary faith and faithfulness, even he struggled mightily and wanted an explanation from God. So God said to Job; *"Shall the faultfinder contend with the Almighty?"* (Job 40:2).

Paul did not contend with God, however. Paul's heart for Jesus was without end and without condition. Had Jesus asked Paul, *"Do you love me more than these?"* his answer would have been a resounding "YES!" In fact, upon receiving his answer to prayer, Paul said, *"Therefore I will all the more gladly boast of my weakness, that the power of Christ may rest upon me. For the sake of Christ, then, I am content with weakness, insults, hardships, persecutions, and calamities; for when I am weak then I am strong"* (2 Corinthians 12:9-10).

Paul remained faithful despite the affliction he suffered. Yet Peter, in a crisis, denied the Lord. Was Peter's heart for Jesus less than Paul's? Was his capacity to serve Jesus inferior to Paul's? Was his impact for the Kingdom of God weaker than Paul's? Of course it was not. Both served Jesus. Both performed miracles in His name. Both gave Him the glory. Both lived for Him and died for Him. Both were made new by Him.

Both were a blessing to Him. Both testified He is Lord and Son of God.

Paul said,

> *Paul a servant of Jesus Christ, called to be an apostle, set apart for the Gospel of God which He promised beforehand through His prophets in the Holy Scriptures, the Gospel concerning His Son who was descended from David according to the flesh and designated Son of God in power according to the Spirit of holiness by His resurrection from the dead, Jesus Christ our Lord, through whom we have received grace and apostleship to bring about obedience to the faith for the sake of His name among all the nations, including yourselves who are called to belong to Jesus Christ* (Romans 1:1-6).

Peter said,

> *For we did not follow cleverly devised myths when we made known to you the power and coming of our Lord Jesus Christ, but we were eye witnesses of His Majesty. For when He received honor and glory from God the Father and the voice was borne to Him by the Majestic Glory, "This is my beloved Son, with whom I am well pleased," we heard this voice borne from Heaven, for we were with Him on the holy mountain. And we have the prophetic word made more sure. You will do well to pay attention to this as to a lamp shining in a dark place, until the day dawns and the morning star rises in your hearts* (2 Peter 1:16-19).

Are we paying attention? Do we serve for the sake of His name? If we love Jesus, we do.

Some may say, "That's not fair." After all, many of us have a lot of responsibilities and our time is short. Just because our plate is full does not mean we love Jesus less than someone who has more time.

If we see it that way, we have missed the point of the question. Jesus did not say, "I know you are busy so whatever time you can give me will be fine." He said, *"Do you love me more than these?"* We all have experience making time for our priorities. Perhaps it is our grandparent, parent, sibling, spouse, child, friend, church, work, school, athletics, performing arts, causes, activities or any one of a number of other possibilities that occupy and inspire our spirit. We pay attention and engage with them in meaningful ways because they matter to us; otherwise, we would do something else with our time.

In some cases, what we are passionate about (say photography) does not pay the bills (yet), so we must do something else. That does not mean that we fail to watch for, to be inspired by and to take a picture of a beautiful sunrise. Granted, it may not mean as much to our family and friends as it does to us, but they are not the reason photography is our great joy and fulfillment. So we take the camera with us and are thankful for moments we are given to capture a picture of the glory of God which we are blessed to see.

The truth is, our time is short. Unless we pay attention to this and serve for His name now, many blessings from God that are available to us may be overlooked in all the activities of our daily routines.

Job put it this way. *"Lo, He passes by me, and I see Him not; He moves on, but I do not perceive Him"* (Job 9:11).

Blessings pass us by without us even knowing. That sunrise or person, and that word or deed, is only ours for a little while. If we think there will always be another sunrise and another opportunity, we have decided that whatever it is, or whoever it is, does not rise to a level that warrants our attention now. If that is the case, that blessing we overlook is unlikely to be important to us tomorrow or the next day.

Love is the point: it pays attention now and it serves where we are in some way until the day dawns and the bright and morning star, Christ Jesus, rises in our heart.

To know Jesus' love is to see it in the beauty of the sunrise; to receive it in each blessing and challenge of the day; and to be saved by it through faith. For without it, one sunrise is pretty much like the next; our blessings and hardships occur without understanding or thanksgiving; and the glory of God in a loved one's passing or healing, or in our own well-being or decline, is missed. In contrast, with Jesus' love there is grace, mercy, peace, hope, strength and purpose for today and for tomorrow.

Confirming our love for Jesus is not difficult. We hear it in our speech and see it in our choices. We experience it in our thoughts and actions. We hold onto it in faith and share it in faithfulness. The motive is love for Jesus, even when we fail Him and do not understand what is happening in our lives. The

Psalmist wrote, *"Let the words of my mouth, and the mediation of my heart be acceptable in thy sight, Oh Lord, my Rock and my Redeemer"* (Psalm 19:14).

When our Lord asked, *"Simon, son of John, do you love me more than these?"* Jesus used his old name, Simon, instead of Peter, the new name Jesus gave him. Was this because Peter had fallen out of favor with Jesus? Did he lose what he had gained through his faith in Jesus? Was it because he had returned to his old self and old ways? Or, was it to reveal that Peter's heart was changed and that his desire was to trust and to follow Jesus?

When we are made new by the Holy Spirit, we honor and acknowledge Christ Jesus as Lord of all, *"to the Glory of God the Father"* (Philippians 2:11). Though we stumble and fall along the way, we do not fall from His grace, or lose what we have gained, or return to what we were for Jesus *"cleansed us from our old sins"* (2 Peter 1:9). In Christ, we are forgiven. We are loved.

CHAPTER 2

For Love

The ones we love most are usually the ones we know best. Something similar can be said of those we dislike. We seem to know quite a lot about them too, or so we think. So, whether we are close to someone or there is a wide chasm between us, there is familiarity. It is the basis of what we believe and how we live.

Our belief gives rise to what we expect. What we expect determines how we prepare. How we prepare influences what we learn. What we learn guides our choices and actions. Our actions reveal who we trust. Who we trust affirms to whom we belong. Who we belong to is reflected in what we do.

Being familiar with the Lord Jesus may begin early in life thanks to someone who loves Him and us, like our parents or grandparents. As a young person it may be our pastor, Sunday school teacher or an evangelist. Later in life it could be our spouse, child or a friend. Perhaps it is someone we meet only briefly whose heart shines with the Spirit of Jesus. Though each one is a blessing, it is God the Father and God the Holy Spirit who know Jesus best and who make Him known to us through the Word of God inspired by the Spirit of God. It is the Holy

Bible that reveals the identity, purpose, power and incomparable love of Christ Jesus:

In the beginning was the Word, and the Word was with God, and the Word was God. He was in the beginning with God, all things were made through Him, and without Him was not anything made that was made (John 1:1-3).

And the Word became flesh and dwelt among us, full of grace and truth, we have beheld His glory, glory as of the only Son from the Father (John 1:14).

And from His fullness have we all received grace upon grace (John 1:16).

The next day he saw Jesus coming toward him, and said "Behold, the Lamb of God, who takes away the sin of the world!" (John 1:29).

I am the bread of life (John 6:35).

I am the light of the world (John 8:12).

I am the door of the sheep (John 10:7).

I am the good shepherd (John 10:11).

I am the resurrection and the life (John 11:25).

I am the way, the truth, and the life (John 14:6).

I am the true vine (John 15:1).

The Word of God and the Spirit of God are active in all who have faith in the Son of God. For without the Father, the Son, and the Holy Spirit, the Word of God may seem to be just another book—more closed than opened, more tiresome than thrilling, more absent from our thoughts than a daily part of them. Within its pages are found:

- The glory and power of God
- The heart of God
- The prophesy of God
- The incarnation of God
- The will of God
- The redeeming love of God
- The call of God
- The providence of God
- The prayer of God
- The offering of God
- The promise of God
- The faithfulness of God
- The sovereignty of God
- The warning of God
- The judgment of God
- The plan of God
- The Son of God, Christ Jesus

Familiarity that involves love is more than knowledge, just as our devotion to family and friends is more than knowledge; just as our capacity to discern thoughts, words, deeds and spirits is more than knowledge; just as our growing in service, wisdom and understanding is more than knowledge; and just as loving, trusting and glorifying Jesus as Lord of all is more than knowledge.

Familiarity that yields this kind of love comes from a relationship that is true, faithful, joyful, thankful and passionate. Truth is its foundation, faithfulness its union, joyfulness its fruit, thankfulness its heart and passion its life. What we are passionate about is what inspires us and fulfills us. We commit to it like nothing else, and we work for it like nothing else. With passion comes love. With love comes abundant life.

Jesus said, *"The thief comes only to steal and kill and destroy; I came that you may have life, and have it abundantly"* (John 10:10). Jesus gives life. He does not steal, kill and destroy. But why did the Lord say "you may have life" instead of "you will have life"? Our life now and life to come depends on who we believe and follow: the source of life or the thief.

If we have the love of Jesus in us, we live and share the love of Jesus through us, as best we can, by the power of the Holy Spirit within us. In relationship with Jesus, we see beyond today and trust the future to Him. Without Jesus, we have no assurance of what will happen when all that we love and trust in the world is gone.

Lifetime Testimony

The book of Job is a testimony of love, faith, tragedy and restoration. After losing all of his worldly possessions and his children, Job said, *"Naked I came from my mother's womb, and naked shall I return; the Lord gave, and the Lord has taken away; blessed be the name of the Lord"* (Job 1:21). Job loved

God and believed God was the source of everything in his life: the blessings, the afflictions, and the life to come. Job saw beyond today and understood the sovereignty of God and, even though his heart was broken, he blessed the name of the Lord.

Job lived his life for God and suffered because of his love for God. What Job did not know was the source of his affliction was the thief, not God. The thief thought that Job would curse God if he lost the blessings and protection of God. God knew that was not so and allowed the thief access to Job. Job did not understand why he was suffering, or by whose hands he was suffering, but he did not fulfill the thief's expectation and curse God. Ultimately, God restored and increased all that was entrusted to Job's care.

Everything God does is for our good (see Romans 8:28). When He disciplines us (like a father disciplines his child) it is not for our harm or destruction, but for our well-being, faith, wisdom and growth.

In the Garden of Gethsemane, as Peter reached for a weapon to defend Jesus from those who came to deliver Him to be condemned and crucified, He said *"Put your sword into its sheath; shall I not drink the cup which the Father has given me?"* (John 18:11). The Lord could have encouraged Peter to take up arms and fight. He could have rallied a multitude to His aid. He could have rioted, set fires, revolted, desecrated monuments and captured the headlines. He could have, but that would not have been of God nor would it have protected us and delivered us from hate, violence and death. It would not have fulfilled the will of God, for Jesus came that we might be reconciled to

God and conformed to His likeness, not to the likeness of the one who steals, kills and destroys.

For His love of humanity Christ Jesus gives life, defends life, prays for life and makes life new. Those who are His have His love in them for the unborn and the elderly, for the Jew and Gentile, for the believer and unbeliever, for the oppressed and the privileged, for the guilty and innocent, for the weary and strong, for the unkind and merciful, for the grieving and joyful, for the sojourner and the neighbor and for the foe and the friend. The Lord said, *"By this all men will know that you are my disciples, if you have love for one another"* (John 13:35).

There is discipline, dilemma, consequence and power in these words. How could Joseph love his brothers after what they did to him (see Genesis 45:4, 45:15)? How could Noah obey God's Word, even though no one but his family heeded what he said (see 2 Peter 2:5)? How could the power of Jesus be received and magnified by a remarkable woman of faith (see Luke 8:47)? How could Stephen pray for those who were stoning him to death (see Acts 7:59-60)?

Each one believed, followed and loved the Lord and each one had the discipline to keep God's Word for God's glory. Discipline is more than steadfastness or being built-up; it is being a disciple. Stephen shared his testimony as he was dying. Joseph shared all that God gave to his care with his brothers. Noah shared God's Word for more than 100 years, even though his countrymen did not believe. A remarkable woman shared her powerful testimony, even while trembling with fear before a large crowd and her Lord. Discipline produces discipleship.

Discipline Produces Outcomes

How do we possess discipline in our ways and words without submitting to discipline? The dilemma is we do not recognize Godly discipline if we do not recognize our need for it. If what we see in the mirror is the last person we would suspect of being unkind, destructive, wrong, and in desperate need of help; then we believe the problem (whatever it may be) is not in ourselves but in someone else. We pass judgment and claim to know the motives of others rather than examining our own motives and confessing our own faults. Even if we do admit that we have accountability for our sins, submitting ourselves to the authority and discipline of another is unlikely unless we agree with them and our spirit is becoming more like them. By becoming more like someone else, we become less like who we have always been, so our old friends may treat us differently. They sense, as we do, that we no longer "fit in" because we are not the same as we used to be. Discipline produces change.

The consequence is not only relational; it is functional. We behave differently. Our values change. Our prayers change. We represent, defend and serve in new ways. We are entrusted with different gifts from God. We suffer and give thanks for that to which we previously gave little or no thought. These changes are not the source of our new focus; they are the effect of our new focus. Discipline produces focus.

The source is God's love and His purpose: that we believe, repent and live, for His judgment is coming (see 2 Peter 3:9-10).

Why is there judgment where there is love? It is from love that there is judgment. What parent would not speak guidance to their child for their child's well-being? What parent would be idle or even complicit rather than discipline their child when their child's life is at risk? What parent would not seek their child's eternal blessing and salvation?

There is judgment because there is love. The absence of judgment does not indicate love — it indicates indifference.

The Father of us all speaks, disciplines, blesses and judges because He loves. We may choose (like children do) to keep or to break His Word, but it is only in keeping it that we come to know the "*hope to which He calls us, the inheritance He has prepared for us, and His immeasurable power in us who believe, according to the working of His great might which He accomplished in Christ when He raised Him from the dead and made Him sit at His right hand in the Heavenly places*" (Ephesians 1:19-20).

If our call is to serve and champion what Jesus has entrusted to our care for His glory and our spirit reflects even a glimpse of His Spirit, then we affirm it is from Him, for Him and by Him that we share His love with someone with whom He connects us by His providence and for His purpose. This discipline is rooted in faith. It is the power of Jesus' life and love in our life, and in our love.

The apostle Paul, inspired by the Holy Spirit, wrote these words, "...*that Christ may dwell in your hearts through faith; that you, being rooted and grounded in love, may have power to comprehend with all the saints what is the breadth and length and height and depth, and to know the love of Christ which*

surpasses knowledge, that you may be filled with all the full-
ness of God" (Ephesians 3:17-19).

To surpass knowledge may seem counterintuitive. After all, we
believe that what we study, practice and achieve occurs due to
our own fortitude, determination and intellect. Yet Paul says
that Christ dwells in our hearts through faith, not fortitude. To
have Christ and to know His great love is not something we can
make happen by our power; it is what the Holy Spirit makes
happen by His power. To be *"filled with the fullness of God"*
is not an achievement of our doing; it is a gift given to us from
love, to love and for love. By it, we comprehend Christ's love.

Without it, we do not have the power to comprehend His love.
Without it, we are not in Christ. Without it, we are moving farther away from Christ. If Jesus is not in us, then something else
is; something that does not receive Him or "love Him more
than these."

Whatever it is fills the place in our spirit that would belong
to Christ. Though we may not call it by its name, we know
its identity because our thoughts are filled with it. Our views
reflect it. Our desire is for it. Our time is devoted to it. Our
deeds serve it. Our words exalt it. Our heart trusts it. Our steps
follow it, and our life belongs to it.

That we belong to someone or something may be difficult to
accept, especially for all of us who esteem our individuality and
freedom as what sets us apart from those who follow someone.
Even if that is our view, however, it confirms that we belong to
the group with this point of view. The truth is we all belong to

something and choose to give ourselves to it, even if it is the belief that we do not belong to anything.

To Whom Do We Belong?

We all need to be connected with someone who values us, stands with us and cares for us. They give their heart and their help to us, and we do not want to let them down.

Whether we are eight or eighty years-of-age, our heart's desire is to be a blessing to them and to thank them for being a blessing to us. They are the ones to whom we belong, by whom we live and grow, and for whom we serve.

A parent wants their child to have absolute assurance that they belong and are loved. No parent wants their child to suffer rejection or persecution. Likewise, no parent wants to suffer tears of separation from the child their arms held, their hands lifted up, their eyes delighted in, their hearts adored and their prayers were for even before they were born. It is an unbearable sorrow to have your child mistreated, as it is to be rejected by the child you cherish.

The Spirit of God the Father indwells the Spirit of God the Son. Jesus affirmed this when He said, *"Truly, truly, I say to you, the Son can do nothing of His own accord, but only what He sees the Father doing; for whatever He does, that the Son does likewise"* (John 5:19). The works, words, mercy, grace, love, suffering and joy of the Lord Jesus are the same as the Father's, and the Father's the same as the Son's.

The Father indwells His children today as well, through their faith in Christ Jesus. Children still emulate their parents' spirit, words, works and ways. God designed the family this way, that it may be a place of learning and blessings by His leading and by our obeying.

Some say this is the basis of our problems so they teach children that what their parents' believe, say, and teach is misinformed, untrue or simply wrong.

Nevertheless, parents' DNA and heart shows up in countless ways in and through their children; in a thought, a mannerism, a word, or a kindness, decision or prayer. Although it may be mocked or frowned upon by those who do not know the parent or who have no interest in the parent, these are great blessings to the children who do.

By God's grace, children grow up to become a conduit of the Father's blessings to someone in their life; because what we learn and keep is what we manifest through our life. God's family is the foundation for what we learn. By His family we recognize the many blessings God gives us, and with our family we give thanks for them. Or we may mock God or be offended by His Word because that is the view of our family, or someone to whom we have given our heart and to whom we belong.

Blessing God

The apostle Paul said, *"Blessed be the God and Father of our Lord Jesus Christ, who has blessed us in Christ with every spiritual blessing in the Heavenly places even as He chose us in Him before the foundation of the world, that we should be holy and blameless before Him"* (Ephesians 1:3-4). This Scripture explains that God has blessed us with spiritual blessings in Christ and it indicates that we are to bless God.

How do we do that? Recognizing our Father has blessed us "in Christ" is the place to start. We are in Christ; in other words, we are a part of His being, a part of His Spirit, a part of His glory by God's blessing and Spirit who indwells us and who exalts Christ Jesus in us. If exaltation of Jesus as the King of kings and Lord of lord's is missing from our heart and from our life, we are not in Christ. Being in Christ is more than being around Him, aware of Him, liking Him, studying Him or even saying, "He is the Son of God, God incarnate, our Savior and Lord, who at this moment is seated at the Father's right hand interceding for us and waiting to return to the world at the Father's command."

Grace, Faith, Love

If we are indifferent to Christ — to the Gospel of His life, death, burial and resurrection — we are not in Christ. We cannot be in Christ if we do not believe Christ. If we are in Christ we rejoice and hope in His Word; we thank Him and praise Him; we trust Him and serve Him; we pray for one another as He does; we know He is God, the Son, the source and reason of all that is entrusted into our care; we honor and share Him as best we can; and we seek to love Him more.

How is it possible to love Jesus more unless we love Jesus now?

How can we love Jesus more unless we know Jesus more?

How can we love Jesus more unless we are changed by His love for us?

Only by grace through faith, from infinite and eternal love, can our love increase for Christ Jesus, to the Glory of God the Father. The way is grace; the heart is faith; the love is God.

Jesus' question *"Do you love me more than these?"* is intimately connected with our love for the Father. To love Jesus like the Father does, with all of His heart, we must have the Father's heart in us. To love the Father as Jesus does, with all of His heart, we must have the Son's heart in us. To love one another more like the Holy Spirit — with forgiveness, mercy, grace and forbearance — we must have the Holy Spirit's heart in us.

This condition of the heart is not something we inherit from our parents or grandparents. It is given by God, the Holy Spirit, to share and apply in our interactions with each other. Chances are we have all had multiple occasions to share God's love, yet we did not, acting instead as if we do not know God and as if His Spirit is not in us.

What must this do to the Spirit of God, to have His children behave as if they have not learned anything from Him, as if they have no thought of Him, and as if they are not a part of Him?

We may have a glimpse of its impact on God by remembering how Jesus answered His disciples, who thought they should bring fire down from Heaven upon Samaria. Jesus said to them, *"You do not know what manner of Spirit you are of"* (Luke 9:55). We may see it in how Jesus wept over Jerusalem. He said, *"You did not know the time of your visitation"* (Luke 19:44). We may experience it when we fail to follow Jesus. He said, *"Will you also go away?"* (John 6:67). We may understand it best by not loving Him. Jesus said, *"If God were your Father, you would love me, for I proceeded and came forth from God; I came not of my own accord, but He sent me"* (John 8:42).

Not knowing the Spirit we are of, being unaware of Jesus' presence with us, leaving Him, and denying our love for Him all shed light on its impact on our Lord.

Blessing Jesus comes from a heart that loves Jesus. David put it like this:

> *Bless the Lord, O my soul; and all that is within me, bless His Holy name! Bless the Lord, O my soul, and forget not all His benefits, who forgives all your iniquity, who heals all your diseases, who redeems your life from the Pit, who crowns you with steadfast love and mercy, who satisfies you with good as long as you live so that your youth is renewed like the eagles. The Lord works vindication and justice for all who are oppressed. He made known His ways to Moses, His acts to the people of Israel. The Lord is merciful and gracious, slow to anger and abounding in steadfast love. His way will not always chide, nor will He keep His anger forever. He does not deal with us according to our sins, nor requite us according to our iniquities. For as the Heavens are high above the earth, so great is His steadfast love toward those who fear Him; as far as the east is from the west, so far does He remove our transgressions from us. As a father pities his children, so the Lord pities those who fear Him. For He knows*

our frame; He remembers that we are dust. As for man, His days are like grass; he flourishes like a flower of the field; for the wind passes over it, and it is gone, and its place knows it no more. But the steadfast love of the Lord is from everlasting to everlasting upon those who fear Him, and His righteousness to children's children, to those who keep His covenant and remember to do His commandments. The Lord has established His throne in the Heavens, and His Kingdom rules over all. Bless the Lord, O you His angels, you mighty ones who do His Word, harkening to the voice of His Word! Bless the Lord, all His hosts, His ministers that do His will! Bless the Lord, all His works, in all places of His dominion. Bless the Lord, O my soul (Psalm 103).

The Lord renews our life like the eagles. He does not deal with us according to our sins. He remembers His children are dust. David exhorted all of God's angels who harken to do His Word, all of His hosts and ministers that do His will, and all of His works in all of His dominion to "Bless the Lord!"

All of His hosts include His children, those who keep His covenant and His commandments. This should not surprise any of us, for even in our daily relationships with family, friends and acquaintances we have a covenant (an agreement) that is the foundation of our interactions with one another; we have commandments (rules) that provide the framework for what we do and believe. The covenant brings us together; commandments keep us together.

So it is with the family of God: the covenant gives us eternal life through faith in Christ Jesus. The commandments give us direction for living life in Christ Jesus.

Evidence that we understand this and that it matters to us is apparent in our reaction to breaking the commandments, which we have all done. Are we more concerned about how this affects us or how it affects God?

If our focus is self we may overlook, or not believe, that our Father suffers when we disobey and dishonor Him. If that is so, we do not understand His great love for us. If we understand and treasure His love for us, we grieve when we grieve Him. Whether we continue the behavior that hurts Him, or stop, depends on who we love most.

Our answer to the question *"Do you love me more than these?"* refers to more than affection; it is the outpouring of our focus and our faith. If our focus and faith are in ourselves, then we promote our own interests, seek our own benefit, and do whatever is necessary to succeed even if it means lying, cheating and stealing. Although we may want and need others to help us accomplish our goals, they are neither the reason nor the motive of our self-interest and self-esteem.

Understanding this is vital to our interactions and affections. When Jesus is our focus and our Lord, He becomes the reason, inspiration, guide, goal, and the glory in what we do. Other things we think, do and say may complement this focus, but they do not rule or reign in His place. That honor belongs to Jesus alone.

Being in Christ gives us insight into His Spirit, like being a part of our family and friends gives us insight into their spirits. Insight that yields understanding and love is the result of being in a relationship. Our insight is superficial at best and in error at worst, without being in relationship. Where love exists, there is a connection that is independent of circumstances and even sorrows. It encompasses faithfulness to endure and a spirit focused on protecting, serving, and blessing what is in our care.

In our relationship with Jesus, we gain understanding of His incomparable love. We rejoice in it, give thanks for it, and share it more and more; although we may not live that way until we begin to love that way.

Being in Christ is being in love with Christ, which is why our answer to His question, *"Do you love me more than these?"* depends on our relationship with Him. It yields understanding, decision and faithfulness.

Faithfulness comes from loving Jesus more, not from our circumstances. Faithfulness is more than believing—it is living what we believe and living in whom we believe.

We believe Jesus and follow Him. Yet believing we are following Jesus while disobeying or disputing His way is a self-deception. The source of the deception is something or someone who does not love Jesus, no matter how much they may profess to do so. Whoever it is wants those who follow Jesus to question what Jesus said, what He meant, what He did, and to turn from Him to follow someone or something else. Faithfulness does not turn away; it follows Jesus.

Anything we or others say or do that hurts Jesus, hurts us. If Jesus is who we love, then we want to be a blessing to Him, not a cause for His suffering or His tears.

We experience this in our daily life with family, friends, teammates, employers, customers, groups we support and in the love of our country. Our desire is for their well-being and their continuance, so we stand with them, serve them, protect them and remain faithful to them, even while suffering with and for them.

For love is not only about here and now. It is:

- understanding sacrifices love has made for us;
- respecting hardships love has endured for us;
- rejoicing in blessings love has won for us;
- keeping faith with love provided for us;
- passing on precepts love has taught us;
- abiding in the security love has acquired for us;
- giving thanks for the gifts love has entrusted to us;
- and ensuring they are available and shared with our loved ones and all whom we are blessed to serve.

Yet, a spirit void of thanksgiving and love soon forgets or discards the source of the gifts and the great price that was paid for them.

Knowing which is worse — forgetting their source and costs, or dismissing our heritage in favor of the times in which we live — is something we will see clearly when we meet Jesus face to face. This we know, however: Jesus is the same today as He was yesterday and He will be the same tomorrow. His way does not change; His Word does not change; His Spirit does not change; and His Kingdom does not change. He obeys the Father; He glorifies the Father and He brings us to the Father. Then we will know if in our lifetime we understood the source and the great costs of the heritage and gifts He placed into our keeping and whether we were good stewards of them and thankful for them; or whether we contributed to their abandonment and destruction by agreeing with or supporting ideologies and practices that do not.

Imagine how thrilling it will be to hear our Lord say *"Well done!"* (Matthew 25:23). Imagine how devastating it would be to hear Him say *"Depart from me for I do not know you"* (Matthew 7:23).

What Might The Difference Be?

Is it that one believes Jesus is Creator and Sovereign Lord, while another does not?

Is it that one is faithful to Jesus, while another is not?

Perhaps one rejoices in Jesus' glorification, while another does not.

Perhaps one suffers when Jesus suffers, while another does not.

Perhaps one affirms Jesus is the source of all that is in their care and they are accountable to Him, while the other does not.

Perhaps one prays for His leading in their life and in the world, and obeys Him, while the other does not.

Is it that one confesses their sins and departs from them, while another does not?

Is it that one shares Jesus' Spirit and love with those they are blessed to serve, while another does not?

Perhaps one understands that what they say and do matters to Jesus, just as what they do not say or do matters, while another does not.

Perhaps it is one whose heart and deeds want to please Jesus, while another's heart does not.

Perhaps one is thankful to Jesus, while another is not.

Perhaps one loves Jesus, while the other does not.

The difference is one is focused on Christ. To be focused on Christ is to be faithful to Christ. For this reason, before we meet Jesus face to face we may have some idea of what He might say to us because we know the motives, deeds, faithfulness and the love we have for Him.

We may say we love Jesus and believe that we do; we may go to church and sing songs that praise and worship Him; we may study and memorize His Word; we may give offerings and we may say prayers for one another; we may know about the warnings of the wrath of God and separation from Him in hell; we may even teach, write, speak, prophesy and serve in His name; and yet we could still hear Him say, *"I never knew you, depart from me, you evildoers"* (Matthew 7:23). How can this be?

How can it be otherwise if our choices and actions reject His Word and dishonor Him? His love for us is not an invitation to do whatever we please. It is a gift for our redemption and rescue. Upon receiving and treasuring it, we turn from following our own way to follow Jesus. We are different than we were before. Moment by moment, day by day, and year by year we are conformed, by the power of the Holy Spirit, to the likeness of Jesus. We become like the one we follow.

Perhaps we have not given much thought to this or to the question *"Do you love me more than these?"*, because it seems intuitive. Of course, we are not the same as we used to be and of course, we love Jesus. Yet, we may admit there is little about the way we interact with each other that is like Jesus. What an unlikely and improbable combination this is, to say we love Him more than anything in our lives, yet not be more like Him in our lives.

Jesus revealed the trouble with a paradox like this when He replied to people who said He was not of God, but of evil, and was casting out evil by the power of evil. Jesus said to them, *"If a kingdom is divided against itself, that kingdom cannot stand. And if a house is divided against itself, that house will not be able to stand"* (Mark 3:24-25). What an amazing way to say that unfaithfulness ends in ruin.

Jesus warned His disciples to *"Take heed that no one leads you astray"* (Matthew 24:4). Who we choose to follow and support is key. We can be led astray from Jesus and from conforming to His likeness and His Word, even while thinking we are being faithful to Him and believing we are standing with Him and serving Him. Why would Jesus say, *"Depart from me"* if we were faithful to Him?

Jesus warns us for a reason. The reason is our salvation.

We have free will to heed the warning, ignore the warning, or reject the warning. However, the reason for the warning does not change. The truth of the warning does not change. The outcome of ignoring or rejecting the warning does not change.

What about mercy, grace, forgiveness and God's love? What about another chance? What about all the deceit, corruption and manipulation we are susceptible to and may not have understood? What about all the good we did? What about kindnesses we extended? What about our prayers? What about the glory we gave? What about the difference we made? What about the love we shared? What about the criticism, rejection and heartache we endured? Doesn't any of that matter to our salvation?

Everything about God matters and everything we do with all God gives us matters, too. Our free will, our decision, our spirit, our faithfulness, our passion, our words, our actions, our love is all our doing. Blaming God for the outcome of choices we make and their impact on our lives, family, community, country and church is wrong. Whether His warnings are heeded and His gifts are protected and served is up to us.

If we bear no resemblance to God, no likeness to His Spirit, no trust in Him, no fellowship with Him, and no obedience to His Word, those are choices we make. We may even receive encouragement and support from others who say, "It doesn't matter if our choices honor God."

If it doesn't matter; if it's all good, why does Jesus say, *"Well done"* to some and, *"Depart from Me"* to others; unless our faithfulness, or lack of faithfulness, does matter to God?

The one we love most is the one to whom we are most faithful. This is the relationship in which we grow, for which we serve and to which we yield love and faithfulness. Unfaithfulness damages and breaks the relationships that are most important to us. When the door is closed and locked, we are separated from the one who matters most. Faith given and kept opens the door; unfaithfulness closes it.

The only thing that changes this is the heart on the other side of the door, in response to knowing the truth of our heart.

Thank God, our mighty Savior Christ Jesus knows our heart. If we truly turn away from what separates us from Him (unfaithfulness to Him), by His mercy and grace the door is opened and we are welcomed in. What if we could do the same as our Savior does for us in our broken relationships with one another?

That would seem to be natural for all who are in Christ. How can one who is in Christ not long to do what Christ does? The person who is in Christ wants Jesus' Spirit at work in their life and wants to please and honor Him with their thoughts, choices, words and deeds. Anything that fails to do so brings a sorrowful and convicting awareness in their spirit as to how far they are from keeping His Way and His Word. It brings a faith-filled response and resolve within their spirit to follow Him closer. If this does not happen, the distance between us and the Lord is farther than we thought. Not to be made new by His Spirit and by His leading is possible only if His Spirit is not in us.

Even though many people all over the world are made new by the Spirit of God, no one is without sin. That we all sin may be in conflict with the opinion we have of ourselves and of our family and friends. If we believe we are without sin, then why give any thought or credence to it? We believe we are fine the way we are. If God made us the way we are and He approves of all we do, then why did Jesus say, *"Truly, truly, I say to you, unless one is born anew, he cannot see the kingdom of God"* (John 3:3). If we think we are fine the way we are, and there is no sin in us, it is unlikely we have been born anew.

Not recognizing our sin; nor being grieved by our sin; continuing to do and to be what we have always done and been; having no need for a Savior because we can manage on our own; and not loving Jesus more than ever before is reason to question if we have been born anew.

When we are born anew we love Jesus with all of our heart, we know He is our Savoir and we know that we desperately need Him to save us. We are not the same as we were, nor do we do what we have always done; we recognize the gravity of our sin and are grieved by it and the sorrow it causes God.

This is by no means an exhaustive list by which we know if we are born anew. The Holy Spirit can reach each us in any way He chooses. Whatever way He chooses will produce a change in our heart, thoughts, priorities, our view and our stewardship of all that is in our care. It will be affirmed by whom we love, follow, glorify, serve and obey. Jesus makes it pretty easy to figure out. He said, *"If you love me you will keep my commandments"* (John 14:15).

There is hope for the future in keeping His commandments today. He is the Good Shepherd and will never leave us or cast us off, even when we fall and lose our way. His great love searches for, rescues and restores all who are His. *"Not one is lost"* (see John 18:9).

We relate to this remarkable love. We would not abandon our child or cast off or forget our sibling, spouse or friend because they fell or lost their way. We even search for and rescue beloved pets and precious items we misplace and rejoice when they are found. Jesus, who is our Creator, defender and propitiation loves us so much more than this, and rejoices so much more when we are together with Him. There is rejoicing in Heaven, too (see Luke 15:10).

It is amazing to think that angels rejoice when we are born anew and love Christ Jesus with all our heart. It would be one thing for people we know to rejoice over our salvation—but Heaven! More than all of our family, friends and acquaintances combined in a "country" more vast than anything we have ever imagined.

Being front page news on every publication in the world would likely pale in comparison to the scope of distribution and jubilant reaction to the news in Heaven of one lost soul being reunited with our Lord.

What is the basis of such celebration? The Gospel of Luke gives us a parable of the spirit of a woman who had lost a coin. She searched her whole house for it, and upon finding it was overcome with great joy, so much so that she invited her friends and neighbors to share the good news and celebrate that what she had lost was found (see Luke 15:9).

Clearly, the coin was highly valuable to her. Maybe she had worked hard for it. Perhaps, someone she cherished had given it to her. What we know for sure is that she treasured it. Little wonder that she searched diligently for it and rejoiced so enthusiastically when it was with her again.

We may be able to relate to her experience if we have lost something of great value then found it and rejoiced over its recovery, and shared the good news with family and friends.

Jesus treasures us so much more than anyone in our lives ever has or ever will. So much so that He willingly took our place and suffered the punishment for our sins to save us from suffering for them ourselves, and from suffering eternal separation from light, peace, joy and loved ones, and from communion with Him. Little wonder His dominion joins in rejoicing and celebrating one who is so precious and treasured by Him, one who was lost and now is found.

There is no greater reason on earth or in Heaven for celebration than the salvation of a soul.

The occasion of our salvation in Christ Jesus — who gives us life and being — is when we know the source, cost, reason and fulfillment of His love and begin to understand it is not by our power (that we who were lost, are saved), but it is a gift of Jesus' power and love.

We accept it with rejoicing and thanksgiving, living and sharing it for the purpose of encouraging and helping one another; believers and unbelievers alike. God calls each of us to faithfulness, to patience and to love. To share His love and light with someone He blesses us to know is possible only if we have His light and His love in us.

We cannot share what we do not have; we cannot accept or apply what we reject and ignore; we cannot be faithful to, or reflect who we do not know and follow; and we cannot glorify Jesus if what we do, say and think does not reflect His Spirit and His Word.

Our love for Christ Jesus is evidenced by how we manifest the content and the spirit of our heart. Our relationships with one another testify to our focus and motives. Our recognition and protection of the sacred stewardships entrusted to our care testify to their source and purpose.

With the love of Christ in us, the love of Christ works through us. His incomparable love inspires and motivates our love for one another and magnifies the reason, the privilege and the accountability we have for all that is in our care. Our pride is then replaced with our prayers, and self-interest gives way to the interests of Christ Jesus.

With Jesus as our Lord and Savior and greatest love, our motive shifts from love of self to love of Him; from our agenda to His. What we once did, and why we did it, compared to what we do now and why we do it may have little in common except this. Then, and now, either His Word and purpose are our focus, or they are not. What we do and think either provides Him glory and honor, or does not. Our love and togetherness with Him either increases, or does not.

Togetherness and faithfulness are fundamental to creating and growing love. Unfaithfulness separates us from each other. We cannot be close to Jesus, or love Him more and profess to follow Him, while being unfaithful to Him.

Unfaithfulness is a wall built stone by stone, day by day and decision by decision. It is not the kind of wall God blessed and directed Nehemiah to build on the borders of Jerusalem that was in accordance with God's Will. The wall of unfaithfulness is of our making and it is a hindrance to our relationship with God.

Unfaithfulness may not seem so bad to the one being unfaithful. We did not mean anything by it; we still love whoever it is and we still want the relationship to continue. We may even believe we have been faithful and that should be good enough.

If we do not expect or care if the one we are in a relationship with is faithful to us, perhaps it is good enough; but if it does matter to the one to whom we are unfaithful to, then it is not good enough. What they say will matter to us only to the degree that we truly love them, that we understand their heartbreak over what we have done, take responsibility for it and are broken ourselves for the suffering we have caused them. What they say will change us only to the degree that we agree with them. Unless we turn from who, or what, we were unfaithful with and return to the one we claim to treasure most of all, we will likely be unfaithful again.

We give our heart, soul and mind to the one we treasure above all.

There was a lawyer who asked Jesus, *"Teacher, which is the great commandment in the law?"* Jesus said to him, *"You shall love the Lord your God with all your heart, and with all your soul, and with all your mind"* (Matthew 22:36-37).

Our heart, soul and mind are who we are and they determine what we do. The heart inspires the motive, the soul inspires the spirit, and the mind inspires the thoughts. When motive, spirit and thought are focused on Jesus, we love Him more; we keep His Word and acknowledge Him at home, work, school, church, in relationships and in our stewardship.

We do this not only because it is the great commandment, but because our Lord showed us what it looks like by living it Himself every day of His earthly life. His motive was to provide a way to salvation. His Spirit was humble, merciful, grace-filled, thankful and obedient. His thoughts were always for God's Will, God's glory and God's love.

Although this is only a glimpse of our Lord and Savior's eternal heart, it offers us a glimpse into our own heart. It prompts us to consider what of God's motive, Spirit and thought indwells us.

Jesus made it easy for us to evaluate the content of our heart. He said, *"If a man loves me he will keep my word, and my Father will love him and we will come to him and make our home with him. He who does not love me does not keep my words; and the word which you hear is not mine but my Father's who sent me"* (John 14:23-24).

The Word of the Father is in Jesus. Father and Son dwell where their Word dwells. Their Word dwells in all who keep it. All who keep it are loved by the Father. Does this mean all who do not keep it are not loved? No! God loves us all, *"for God so loved the world that He gave His only Son that whoever believes in Him should not perish but have eternal life"* (John 3:16). It means we who love His Word, love His Son, and manifest our love for Him in our relationships with one another.

CHAPTER 3

For One Another

The indwelling Spirit of Christ connects us with one another by His providence and for His purpose. When we deviate from, or fail to serve people, places, times and opportunities that He entrusts to our care, it is not because His Spirit is unwilling or incapable; it is because our doubt, denial and fear keep us from fulfilling His purpose to care for one another in His Spirit.

Our idleness may make His Spirit restless within us, yet His Spirit is faithful and loving, even when ours is weak. When we sense some restlessness in ourselves it may be due to disobedience or pride that limits our understanding, usefulness and progress in serving His purpose.

Apostle Paul

The apostle Paul went from contempt and rejection of Christ to love for Christ and being sent by Christ for our sake. It was Paul who said, *"What you have learned, received, heard and seen in me, do; and the God of peace will be with you"* (Philippians 4:9). Paul would know because the peace of God was within him. Paul served Jesus by serving us at great risk to himself. He did this, in part, by loving, obeying, honoring, and living in the Spirit of Christ. First, however, Paul had to receive the

Spirit of Christ; to become filled with the Spirit of Christ; to become useful to the Spirit of Christ for our good.

Our usefulness to Christ may have a lot to do with what Paul advised. "What you have learned—do." The salvation and peace of Jesus indwelled Paul and was lived through Paul by the purpose and power of God. Paul told us what his purpose was: *"the stewardship of God's grace which was given to me for you"* (Ephesians 3:2).

So it is with everyone who loves Jesus and is useful to Him: stewardship is given to us in order to serve one another. The Word of God helps us to know how: Apply what you have learned, received, heard and seen in Christ Jesus, through His Word, His service, and His Spirit, with one another.

James, the half-brother of Jesus said:

> ...*be doers of the Word, and not hearers only, deceiving yourselves. For if anyone is a hearer of the Word and not a doer, he is like a man who observes his natural face in a mirror; for he observes himself and goes away and at once forgets what he was like. But he who looks into the perfect law, the law of liberty, and perseveres, being no hearer that forgets but a doer that acts, he shall be blessed in his doing* (James 1:22-25).

Paul and James learned from, and received, the Lord Jesus and were transformed by His Spirit. Many who knew Paul's former life and James's former opinion of his brother must have pondered what happened to these men to change them. Not only had they become faithful followers of Christ Jesus; they became suffering servants and stewards of His Gospel and His grace for our sake.

At some point we discover that what we have learned, listened to, accepted and believed determines more than our perspective, circumstance and experience: it is what we have sought and who we want.

It is the reason we think the way we do. It is the reason we say what we do. It is the reason we act as we do. It is the reason we support and defend what we do. It is the reason we believe what we do. It is the reason we pray for God's permission and His direction.

It involves serving someone and honoring someone and being someone—for someone. If this is not apparent yet, it will become so because the likeness of who we honor and serve will become our likeness as well. Perhaps we know who it is, perhaps we do not, but we can anticipate that someday we will be more like the one we follow, obey, trust, serve and above all, love.

So, our answer to the Lord's question, *"Do you love me more than these?"* may give us insight into questions about what is yet to be. For example, who are we becoming? Where will we be? What will we be doing and how can we know? Part of the answer is connected to who we are right now.

Is there evidence in the way we treat one another and by the choices we make that we are spending time with Jesus; that we are following Him and that our thoughts and prayers are becoming more like His?

Might the evidence be that some people liked us better when Jesus was not our focus? Could it be that some people get upset by what we think, say and do? Could it be that some people think it is fine to love Jesus, but not too much, and certainly not too publicly or too vocally?

Those may be evidences, but far more important than what someone thinks or says about us is what we think and say about Jesus and what He thinks about us. We have no audience more important than Jesus.

We know that some of those whom He loved and served rejected Him and failed Him. We know that His Spirit is merciful, gracious, humble and forgiving. We know He is faithful and obedient to the Father who sent Him into the world to love us, to serve us and to save us. We know that He makes new all who follow Him and who live *"for the praise of His glory"* (Ephesians 1:12). For this we say, "Thank you, Father, for loving us so much, even when we can be so unloving to one another and unloving to You. You gave Jesus for us, you glorify Jesus in us, and you give us the privilege of serving Jesus and one another through the blessings You entrust to us. For, whatever You give us and allow us to do is possible only by Your presence in us and Your gift of love for us."

God's Word says, *"...My counsel shall stand, and I will accomplish all My purpose..."* (Isaiah 46:10). What a great comfort, especially when we endure hardships, or when a loved one or a friend dies along with so much of what they did; even the many relationships they cherished and impacted seem to die due to their absence. Yet, their service, their purpose, their influence, their spirit, their love, and ours, does not end because their location has changed. God's Word makes it clear that His counsel "stands" and His purpose is "accomplished." His counsel and purpose includes our lives. Jesus affirmed this when He said, *"I am the resurrection and the life; he who believes in me, though he die, yet shall he live, and whoever lives and believes in me shall never die. Do you believe this?"* (John 11:25-26).

Our response to, *"Do you believe this?"* is closely related to our response to, *"Do you love me more than these?"* Giving our heart to someone, loving them above all, requires giving them all of our trust, as well.

Love & Trust

Although we may trust without love, it is impossible to honor God without love and trust. The one we truly love is the one we truly trust.

The Lord's questions, *"Do you believe this?"* and *"Do you love me more than these?"* address the same issue: the condition of our heart for Jesus. For if we truly love Jesus, we truly believe Jesus. If we believe Jesus, what He says is true.

Some of us may disagree on the grounds that there are people in our lives we love who say things that are not true, but we still love them. Our heart for them may even overflow with love, but it does not overflow with trust, because we do not believe what they say.

This argument does not dilute the point that the one we truly love is who we truly trust; it affirms that the point is the condition of our heart for that person. If there is trust, then we believe; if there is not trust, we love, but we do not believe.

Our answer to the question *"Do you believe this?"* is either trusting love, love without trust, or uncertainty. The condition of the heart is the foundation to the answer.

Although we may say we love and believe Jesus, there may be no evidence of that in our choices, behaviors, speech, and how we serve Him and each other. Proof of what we believe is not limited to what we think and say; it is manifested through our love for Jesus, the transformation of our thoughts, decisions and activities. Love that transforms also conforms, day by day, to the power of its source and its presence.

We reflect its source to the degree we are connected to it because who and what we keep in our heart is who and what we reflect in our lives. Some may say, "That is not true" or "We have moved-on." If that is so, then whatever we moved-on from and replaced, we were never really committed to in the first place, because if it had been our source and life we would not have, and could not have moved-on without it. We cannot live apart from our source any more than we can live apart from the air we breathe.

Why do we experience such deep sorrow when our great God's Word and love are rejected? Why do we grieve so profoundly when a loved one passes? Why are we so concerned (even consumed) over our country's elections? It is because our lives are intimately connected with each one. Evidence of this is the great impact and thankfulness we feel upon a visit to Arlington National Cemetery; it is confirmed by the heartfelt joy and memory we have of loved ones we once held in our arms, and long to be with again; and above all, it is lived through us by the great love that leads us, inspires us and saves us: Jesus Christ.

We do not move-on from what connects us: from our heritage, from what we love, protect, honor and serve. Ignoring, or forgetting, the very source of our blessings, privileges and opportunities would be like denying or rejecting our mother, father, family, or country and their great sacrifices and enduring love for us.

If we do not protect, respect and honor the history from which we came and upon which we stand and grow, then those who follow us (our families, friends and all for whom we work and serve) will be unlikely to honor and protect what they came from and upon which their lives stand and grow.

Christ Jesus is our source. The apostle John, inspired by the Holy Spirit, said, *"...all things were made through Him (Jesus), and without Him was not anything made that was made"* (John 1:3). That makes it clear that Jesus gives us life; He gives us one another; He gives us our republic and its Constitution; He gives us our blessings; He gives us our stewardships; He gives us His Word; and He gives us His life. How we honor what He trusts to our care, how we protect and serve it, is related to our love for Him and our love for one another.

The first words of the Bible tell us, *"In the beginning God created the heavens and the earth"* (Genesis 1:1). It does not say God created multiple earths or that there were other sources of creation. His Word does not make reference to multiple sources or a backup plan.

The end of the first chapter of Genesis says, *"And God saw everything that He had made, and behold, it was very good"* (Genesis 1:31). It does not say, "God looked and behold there was jealousy, strife, pride, hate, vengeance, greed and sin." These would be contributed by the caretakers of God's creation, and we are all caretakers. From Adam and Eve to each of us, we are all stewards of His creation.

What we do with our individual stewardship depends on recognizing it as stewardship in our care for a time. It depends on our thankfulness for the privilege Jesus has entrusted to us; it depends on our keeping His Word and His way; and it depends on our daily focus on applying it to serve one another for the glory of God.

By remembering its source, purpose, privilege and outcome, we pray for its fulfillment. The fruit it bears may take time and perseverance, but the love it shares is timeless.

This is not a foreign concept. We experience it in our lives and service to our loved ones, customers, teams, employers and with so many gifts temporarily in our care. It involves recognizing, cherishing and honoring who we come from, who we depend on, and who we love, represent and serve.

Our obedience, spirit and motives say more about our love for them than it does about us. We understand why this is true; we have lived it.

When the one we love is hurt, we suffer with them. When they grieve, we grieve. When they rejoice, we give thanks and rejoice, as well. Our greatest love is our greatest motivation and our greatest joy. They are the spirit, inspiration and power underlying why and how we do what we do.

Our answer to the Lord's question *"Do you love me more than these?"* is the foundation of all we think and do.

Some may say, "My greatest motive is equality, justice and freedom." As worthy and thoughtful as these concepts are, they are not a person. The person we love is the basis of the calling on our heart, and it is for them we serve one another, that what we do may bring them honor and joy.

If what we are doing does not honor them, and it is not their prayer for us, then we may be following and serving someone other than the one we say we love. We cannot bring glory to the one we love by having a spirit at work within us, and through us, which does not honor them or do what they do. That would be like saying Christ Jesus is our greatest love, but not doing or believing what Jesus did and believed. Jesus kept and shared His Father's Word. Jesus obeyed and served His Father's will. Jesus glorified His Father through the words He spoke, the deeds He did and Spirit He embodied. Jesus helped us, prayed for us and gave Himself for us. His Spirit forgives and lifts us up. Those who love Him do what He did and what He does in order to obey and honor God.

The heart of Jesus and the hearts of all who love Jesus rejoice in the glory of God, in the Word of God, in the will of God, in the Spirit of God, in the worship of God, serving and giving thanks for the daily blessings in our care and for the sovereignty and incomparable gift of God—our salvation through grace by faith in the person and the redeeming work of the Son of God,

Christ Jesus, our Lord, Creator and Savior, *"the reason"* for the hope we have (see 1 Peter 3:15).

Our greatest love is our greatest reason. We live our love; and we grow in it, and by it, in all we do for one another.

Bitterness, resentment and malice in our thoughts, words and actions are signs (at least during those moments) that we are not following Jesus, and we are not glorifying Him in our lives. It suggests that we are giving ourselves to someone or something other than Christ and that our fellowship with Jesus has suffered; not because He left us, but because we left Him.

We know this is true because bitterness, resentment, envy, lies and malice are not part of Jesus' Spirit. They are, however, a part of the world's spirit, which can take hold of us and draw us away from Jesus. It is not a matter of whether this happens; but when it happens, how do we respond?

Our response depends on whether or not we remember why we are sent and whether or not our conduct and spirit bears any resemblance to the one to whom we belong. If it does, we keep and apply precepts we have learned.

God's Word teaches that the fruit of the Holy Spirit in us is *love, joy, peace, patience, kindness, goodness, faithfulness, gentleness and self-control* (Galatians 5:22) We may not always exemplify these behaviors, but when they are present in our spirit and our deeds, or we see them in others, we know their source. The fruit of peace and self-control is from the source of peace and self-control; Christ Jesus, the Prince of peace.

Our Lord said, *"Peace I leave with you; my peace I give to you; not as the world gives do I give to you"* (John 14:27). Jesus offers us peace with God, with one another and with ourselves. Why then do we experience so much that is not peaceful in our lives and in our country?

To have the peace Jesus offers, we must receive the peace Jesus gives. We cannot experience it until we have it. We cannot have it until we accept it. We cannot apply it until we live it.

Our reactions to difficulties we experience at home, work, school, and elsewhere indicate that this is easier said than done. How can we be so angry, upset, unforgiving, unkind, and not be at peace, if the peace of Jesus is in us? How can the refreshing sleep and joy that abounds in gratitude be so elusive? How can something that happened weeks, months or even years ago continue to burden our spirit in the present, if we received and have applied the gift of Jesus' peace?

Perhaps we never accepted or truly believed it or applied it in the first place. Perhaps we let our awareness, understanding and use of it be altered by what is outside of us rather than who is inside of us.

Peace

The peace of Jesus does not eliminate the challenges and warnings we face, but it does help us heed them and guide us through them.

The peace Jesus offers is rest from the many burdens we put upon ourselves and that others put upon us. It assures us of

His presence, power, sovereignty and victory. It provides daily direction and blessings while inspiring, renewing and fulfilling our spirit. It brings us to prayer, thanksgiving, praise, worship, joy, learning, growth and sharing. Christ Jesus is the source of peace in our thoughts, words and spirit.

What about all those times when we are without peace? We love the Lord and have His Spirit, but there seems to be no evidence of His presence or His peace working through us, either for ourselves or for the good of people we are blessed to know and serve. In fact, during those times we may be adding our lack of peace to theirs. How can this happen if we have Christ in us?

The spirit of the world is filled with conflict, controversy and unrest. It occupies a part of all of us, for a time, especially during those circumstances in which we allow it. We may even thrive on it, be consumed by it, or let it direct us or exploit us. When this is so, a spirit that is not of Christ has been allowed by us to gain ground. The result is that we may forget, ignore or suppress the Spirit of Christ. This is not because Christ has not given Himself to us; a more likely explanation is that we have not given ourselves to Christ. When we realize this, we turn our thoughts and spirit back to the Lord and find peace in Him, until or unless we let something else draw us away again.

A sure manifestation that we are filled with the world's spirit rather than the Spirit of Christ is when we are so occupied by a conflict, controversy or unrest that our focus is getting even with someone and having our way prevail, no matter what impact or toll it has on someone else; least of all, on those with whom we are in conflict. This was never Jesus' way or His Spirit. When it becomes ours — whether for a moment or for weeks, months or years — we are neither in Christ, nor with Christ, but we are opposed to Him and are actively and willingly serving someone or something other than Him. Jesus did not succumb to the spirit of the world. He overcame it by forgiving, submitting, serving, "*dying for our trespasses and rising to life for our justification*" (Romans 4:25).

Our enmity and conflict with one another is enmity with our Creator and Savior—Christ Jesus. For we do not "love Christ more than these" while a spirit of conflict, controversy and getting even rules our thoughts and deeds. That would be like saying we love and serve Christ, while being filled with rage and hardness of heart toward someone He died to save.

We may justify our unforgiving spirit with thoughts like "they are getting what they deserve", "they brought it on themselves" and the greatest lie of all, "they are unworthy of the love of Christ." However, it is not our grace we withhold and fail to share with someone we are at odds with; it is the grace Jesus freely gave to us while we were yet sinners for our peace, for our faith, and for caring for one another.

> *Therefore, since we are justified by faith, we have peace with God through our Lord Jesus Christ. Through Him we have obtained access to this grace in which we stand, and we rejoice in our hope of sharing the glory of God. More than that, we rejoice in our sufferings, knowing that suffering produces endurance, and endurance produces character, and character produces hope, and hope does not disappoint us, because God's love has been poured into our hearts through the Holy Spirit which has been given to us (Romans 5:1-5).*

The gift of the Holy Spirit is shared through us, not only with those we are close to (because it is easy to be kind to someone who is kind to us), but those with whom we are at odds or who have hurt us. Lest we forget, the point is to apply the gift given to our care, as often as we can, wherever we can, with everyone we can because it is God who informs, inspires and leads us. It is God who opens the doors and provides the opportunities we have to meet one another and to encourage one another. It is God whose Word and power renews and fortifies our spirit. It is God who gives us faith and faithfulness. It is God who makes our progress possible. It is God whose *"face shines upon us and is gracious to us"* (Numbers 6:25).

We may need someone to remind us of this when our focus becomes the rancor and recriminations of our day. It is easy to get caught up in the dissention and let fault-finding and retaliation become the heart of our spirit. Our anger and criticism may not be limited to a person.

If, or when, that happens we may wonder, and even pray, "God, what have You done?" Even Moses had that question. He said. *"O Lord, why hast thou done evil to this people? Why didst thou ever send me?"* (Exodus 5:22).

Our murmurings against God are foolishness. The only one who celebrates it, who is pleased by it, who encourages and fosters it, is the enemy of God. Who but the enemy of God wants to change our allegiance to God; wants to end our usefulness to God; and wants us to question the glory of God and our worship of God? Whatever banner these motives, or motives like them, are under we can be certain it is not from God and it is not for God.

A better question to ask is, "God, what have I done?" or "God, what have we done?" For God gave us life, free will, the Garden of Eden, and He gives us His promise, faithfulness and provisions. His enemy and accuser lead us away from God and replace our love for God and for one another with murmuring, distrust and conflict. Yet we ask, "Why did You do this?" instead of, "Why did we let this happen to us?"

Perhaps we let it happen by ignoring, editing or rejecting God's Word. Perhaps it happened due to pressures and practices of the day to which we surrendered. Perhaps it came from neglecting God, or following after someone or something that lies or is opposed to God, to His Word and to our salvation. Perhaps we have not recognized or acknowledged the source of every blessing in our care. Perhaps we want to blame someone for the conditions, hardships and sorrows of life. Perhaps we have not heard of, or have forgotten or have failed to seek *"God's righteousness and His Kingdom"* (Matthew 6:33). Perhaps what we see and experience are outcomes of choices we have made that do not follow and honor God. Perhaps we expect the worst from one another rather than the best. Perhaps we do not know ourselves, or Christ Jesus, who came to save us from ourselves.

Spiritual Battle

By knowing Jesus better, by following Jesus closer and by loving Jesus more, we come to know and experience the spiritual battle being waged for our soul, the power of the enemy and the price Jesus paid for the victory He won for us.

If there were no combatants, our spirit might never be troubled or hurt; we might never have a great decision to make; we might never have a commitment or a standard to uphold; we might never have someone counting on us to be faithful, trustworthy, willing and available to help. Consider why anyone would commit themselves to fight for us, or against us, unless we have value and make a difference?

Without impact and value there would be no one standing with us, fighting for our victory. Without impact and value there would be no one standing against us, fighting for our defeat.

God's Spirit in us affirms that we do have great value and impact, each one of us: the born and the unborn; the weak and the strong; the young and the old; the courageous and the cautious; the warrior and the peacemaker; the care-receiver and the care-giver.

The more our love and faithfulness reflect our value and service to Jesus, the greater the attack against us will be by those who oppose Jesus. Jesus said, *"Blessed are you when men revile you and persecute you and utter all kinds of evil against you falsely on my account"* (Matthew 5:11).

Later Jesus said:

> *You have heard that it was said, "You shall love your neighbor and hate your enemy." But I say to you, love your enemies and pray for those who persecute you, so that you may be sons of your Father who is in Heaven, for He makes His sun rise on the evil and the good, and sends rain on the just and the unjust. For if you love those who love you, what reward have you? Do not even tax collectors do the same? And if you salute only your*

*brethren, what more are you doing than others? Do not
even Gentiles do the same?* (Matthew 5:43-47).

Jesus not only said these things, He lived them. His love overcame the trials and tribulations of the world that He endured
for our sake.

The power of the enemy against Him was not only a person,
a group and a nation, but everyone throughout time who
rejects His Word, His Sovereignty, His judgment and His love.
The greatness of the power of a whole nation taking aim at
destroying one man may seem unimaginable, but it happened
to Jesus and Jesus told Simon Peter and His disciples that it
would happen to them for their faithfulness to Him. Even so,
Jesus said to Peter and to all who love Him, *"Follow me!"*
(John 21:22).

Jesus answered the question many people had then and have
today. "Why do hate and vengeance even exist and increase
over time?" The Lord said, *"If you were of the world, the world
would love its own; but because you are not of the world, but
I chose you out of the world, therefore the world hates you"*
(John 15:19). Can we imagine being hated by the world for not
following the ways of the world?

The Way We Choose

What if the world chose to approve and support the destruction
of trees — young and old, healthy and weak — not because
they have no value, but because of the water they require, the
air they breathe, the space they take and the care they need?
What if they chose to do this even though there are many who

view trees as a gift and a stewardship from God, entrusted to us by God's providence and for God's purpose?

The motives are vastly different, as are the short and long term outcomes of the two options. Plans are made by each side and great resources required to win the day for their point of view.

In this hypothetical example, the trees are without a voice of their own and without a way to engage in the process and the decision regarding themselves. They rely entirely on someone speaking for them, defending them and loving them. They are literally at the mercy of what the world decides. When the world makes its decision, there is a choice each of us make. We either support the world's choice, or we do not.

Our answer to the Lord's question, *"Do you love me more than these?"* has everything to do with our decision and it is closely associated with how and why we make the decision we do. Our choice reflects and impacts who we love.

How this commitment is applied may be different for each of us, and it depends on how much we love. The place to start is with prayer. Ask for God's guidance and permission, for without it our decision may have nothing to do with God or His will. Remembering and obeying God's Word is another step that helps focus our attention on His Lordship and His heart. Waiting for and responding to His answer may be the most difficult part of the process, because patience requires peace and confidence. In the middle of the decision-making process — especially one that is troubling and calls for courage — peace and confidence may sometimes be difficult to embrace.

Talking with family and friends we love and who love us, and who love Jesus, can be a great comfort and help.

Considering our primary purpose and greatest desire is to be a blessing and a joy to the one we love most, it is difficult for us to fully understand the impact our words and actions have on them; or to recognize and take responsibility for the times we did not take them into consideration. In fact, there are times we gave them no thought at all; and in doing so left them out, let them down and broke their heart.

Perhaps, we have had this experience when a family member or a friend left a loved one out and were unaware of this over-sight's great impact on them. Or perhaps there has been a time we were the cause of leaving someone out, or we were the one forgotten. In each case, there is an impact (possibly for everyone involved) because the greatest joy and greatest sorrow is always connected to the greatest love.

No one embodies this more than Christ Jesus; and no one loves us more than He does. Before we were born, before we knew Him, before we believed and received Him, before we began to follow Him, He loved us, lived for us, died for us, and was resurrected for us. He intercedes for us, defends us, guides us, inspires us, provides for us, blesses us, prays for us and forgives us. He teaches, corrects, enables, fortifies, leads, delivers and keeps us. He is the source of everything entrusted to our care. He is our hope, peace, joy and reward. He goes before us, He is with us and He is for us. He is our life, our light, our atonement and our Savior. He suffers when we suffer, He weeps when we weep and He rejoices when we rejoice.

Imagine His Joy

Imagine His joy when we actively and intentionally keep Him in our thoughts, honor Him by our words, glorify Him with our deeds and exalt Him in our prayers. Imagine His joy when we defend what He defends and cherish and serve all He trusts to our care. Imagine His joy when we share and embody His Spirit, His Word, His way, His mercy, His grace, His humility and His forgiveness. Imagine His joy when we seek His permission, trust His leading and follow Him. Imagine His joy when we remember He is the source of our lives and of all creation. Imagine His joy when we have faith, gratitude, peace and joy in His Spirit. Imagine His joy and love when we meet Him face to face and He welcomes us home and reunites us with our loved ones.

Imagine His broken heart when we do not share and embody His Spirit, His way, and His love. Imagine His sorrow when we do not seek His guidance and trust His leading. Imagine His suffering when we do not remember He is the source of our lives—and of all creation. Imagine His pain when we do not have faith, gratitude, peace and joy in Him. Imagine His tears when we are not reunited with Him and our loved ones. Imagine His anguish when our lives, words, decisions and spirits bear no reflection or remembrance of Him.

This is not difficult to imagine. We know His heart and His great love. We hear it in this prayer, *"Father, I desire that they also, whom thou hast given to me, may be with me where I am, to behold my glory which thou hast given me in thy love for me before the foundation of the world"* (John 17:24). His great love for us was confirmed during the proceedings of His mock trial through the contempt, beatings, scourging, scorn and hate He endured from people He served; by the agony He felt with every step He took on His way to Calvary; and from His willingness to take our place and our suffering so that one day we may be where He is to behold His glory and rejoice in His great love for us.

Little did those who conspired against Jesus know when they said, *"He saved others; but He cannot save Himself"* (Matthew 27:42) that very thing they were doing would actually help achieve the very thing they desperately wanted to prevent: fulfillment of His Word, establishment of His Church and His eternal glorification. The words of their mouth, "He saved others", confirms they knew about the miraculous works He did. "But He cannot save Himself", testified to their failure to understand God's Word given 700 years before Jesus was born. Isaiah prophesied about Him and wrote these words:

Who has believed what we have heard? And to whom has the arm of the Lord been revealed? For He grew up before Him like a young plant, and like a root out of dry ground; He had no form or comeliness that we should look at Him, and no beauty that we should desire Him. He was despised and rejected by men; a man of sorrows, and acquainted with grief; and as one from whom men hide their faces, He was despised and we esteemed Him not. Surely He has born our griefs and carried our sorrows: yet we esteemed Him stricken, smitten by God, and afflicted. But He was wounded for our transgressions, He was bruised for our iniquities; upon Him was the chastisement that made us whole, and we with His stripes are healed. All we like sheep have gone astray; we have turned everyone to his own way; and the Lord has laid on Him the iniquity of us all. He was oppressed, and He was afflicted, yet He opened not His mouth; like a lamb that is led to the slaughter, and like a sheep that before its shearers is dumb, so He opened not His mouth. By oppression and judgment He was taken away; and as for His generation, who considered that He was cut off out from the land of the living, stricken for the transgression of my people? And they made His grave with the wicked and with a rich man in His death, although He had done no violence, and there was no deceit in His mouth. Yet it was the will of the Lord to bruise Him; He has put Him to grief; when He makes Himself an offering for sin, He shall see His offspring, He shall prolong His days; the will of the Lord shall prosper in His hand; He shall see the fruit of the travail of His soul and be satisfied; by His knowledge shall the righteous one, my servant, make many to be accounted righteous; and He shall bear their iniquities. Therefore I will divide Him a portion with the great, and He will divide the spoil with the strong; because He poured out His soul to death, and was numbered with the transgressors; yet He bore the sin of many, and made intercession for the transgressors (Isaiah 53:1-12).

The very thing those who conspired to put Jesus to death thought would ensure His destruction was the very thing God had spoken that foretold Jesus' death, burial, resurrection, glorification and victory. So confident were they who mockingly said, *"He cannot save Himself"*, but how wrong they were who failed to understand that it was not His life He came to save.

It was theirs, and ours and our children's and our children's children and every child in every family and every generation.

God's Word says Christ Jesus created the world (John 1:3); He knew all that was to happen to Him (John 18:4); and that everyone of the truth hears His voice (John 18:37).

The Creator's voice: — speaking truth, knowing our minds and our motives — came into the world, aware of what the world would do to Him, innocent of the crimes He was accused of, yet suffering at our hands (John 19:4) and forsaken in His death (Matthew 27:46). Oh, such love that willingly suffers and dies for another; not just for friends and people who love Him, but for those who hate Him. This is the heart of God: love, forgiveness and salvation for us and for all who believe.

Someone Like That

"One another" is a familiar phrase that may bring to mind a vast number of people, including those with whom and for whom we serve; everyone we know, identify with, support and defend; and many people we have never met, but with whom we share a connection and goal. It is a less common way of thinking about and interacting on a daily basis with people to whom we are not close and to whom we may be opposed; or who have lied about us, or by whose hand or spirit we have suffered. We cannot, and will not, forgive "someone like that", when we are in the right and they are in the wrong. The problem is that we are all "someone like that".

We may not admit it, or believe it, but there are times our spirit has little resemblance to the Spirit of Christ. Perhaps we even resist His Spirit. How must this impact our usefulness to God, to our service for one another and to our prayers? By denying His Spirit, His promptings and His blessing to reach out, to offer forgiveness and kindness to one another, we miss an opportunity to honor God by applying His Spirit of reconciliation and restoration. We miss an opportunity to fulfill the calling our Lord has entrusted to our care: to keep His Word.

It is not a matter of *if* we are "someone like that"; someone who is unkind, unforgiving and who may even return *"evil for good"* (Proverbs 17:13). *When* we are "someone like that", how do we respond? Perhaps we ignore, deny, hide, or justify it. Maybe we choose to forget it or dismiss it as something so uncharacteristic of us we cannot understand or explain it. Or maybe we regret it, repent of it, learn from it and grow closer to Jesus because of it, while asking for His guidance and help to do better with the next opportunity He provides.

How we respond is dependent on everything our Lord means to us and on our understanding of all we mean to Him.

When we give our heart to another it becomes one with theirs, and theirs with ours. We are with each other and for one another; serving, rejoicing and suffering as one. Should this not be so, and we all fall short, the spirit of our response and our words may indicate whether or not we have given our hearts to one another.

Our connection gives us far better understanding of one another than would ever be possible without it. With them in our heart, we may even begin to see like they see; to hear like they hear; to understand like they understand; to feel like they feel; to hope like they hope; to pray like they pray; and to respond like they respond.

Our acknowledgment of the glory of God's creation in earth, sky and sea; to the incomparable love, faithfulness and Lordship of Jesus; to the sacredness of every person's life; to the many gifts of stewardship we are privileged to offer for His glory; to His suffering and resurrection for our rescue and restoration testifies to our love and our heart for Christ Jesus and for one another.

Caring for one another in the Spirit of Jesus may come more easily for those we love and who love us; but Jesus did not reserve His love for only those who loved Him. When we remember this and apply the teaching of Jesus intentionally to our relationships, we draw closer to Christ Jesus and to one another. When we fail to do so, we are not keeping His Word. So how do we know? We know because Jesus said, *"love one another"* (John 13:34).

Our Creator, Sustainer and Savior did not say, "love only those who are nice to you", or "love only those who are helpful to you", or "love only those who agree with you", or "love only those who love you." He said to *"love one another."* This includes those who can be mean-spirited, unforgiving, unhelpful, unjust, and unloving. This includes all of us.

Christ Jesus loved by sharing God's Word, living God's Word, and entrusting God's Word to us. He reached out to us, and He walked with us, called us, served us, taught us and forgave us. He cherishes us and prays for us. He warns, corrects, inspires, and waits for us. He gives sacred stewardships into our care, He helps us, He gives us one another, and He gives us Himself.

He reminds us to first love God and to love one another. He teaches us to follow Him, apply our faith and to pray; to serve one another, forgive one another and to love one another; and with all our ways to remember Him: our Creator, Savior and Lord.

When our service here is complete and we are blessed to be in His glorious presence, we may finally and fully understand His monumental love. We may finally and fully appreciate that all the places, people and times we were blessed to know, to care for, to pray for and to love were from Him. We may finally and fully give Jesus all of our thanks and all of our love for the unsurpassed joy and fulfillment of knowing (in His Spirit, by His power and according to His will) that our love for one another, like His for us, is eternal.

CHAPTER 4

Not Alone

"Jesus wept" (John 11:35).

E manuel—God with us, the Son of God, the Lamb of God, the Lion of Judah, the Lord of lords, the King of kings, the Alpha and the Omega —, wept with and for the family and friends of Lazarus, even though He was about to restore Lazarus to life, call him out from the tomb, and direct those standing nearby to unbind him and let him go (see John 11:44). Even so, the Creator of Heaven and earth wept.

Jesus could have spared Himself their broken hearts. He could have focused on something else. Yet He focused His heart on them, on their suffering and grieving. He did not ignore them or abandon them; He joined them and blessed them and had great love and compassion for them as He does for us.

If that is true, then how do we explain the times we have wondered and felt let down, like the sisters and friends of Lazarus did, concerning the whereabouts of Jesus and why we seem to be crying and suffering alone? It seems as though no one understands what we are going through, or is for us, or with us. But Jesus said, *"I am with you always"* (Matthew 28:20). Do we believe Him? Maybe we are convinced He is not present in our suffering. It is not our power or our perception that makes His promise true, however. It is the unsurpassed love Jesus has for us; His Word to us in the Bible; it is His Spirit in us that makes it true.

The Holy Bible is such a great gift and blessing from God. We may not all agree about what it says or what it means, or its power and purpose, but we can agree on this: there are so many names recorded in Scripture and so many accounts of people, their families, what they did and God's presence in their lives.

Why? What relevance does it have to us? Are names and families listed for reasons of genealogy? Are details provided for historical information? Is the recounting a work of literature, sharing the conditions and outcomes of lives in another time? It is all of these and more.

The Scripture reveals our great God knows and remembers our names; He cares for our lives and our families; He is with us and for us in the times, places and circumstances of our lives. God knows every one of us because He formed each of us in our mother's womb (see Psalm 139:13) and He gave us Himself (see Mark 10:45).

All the gifts and privileges entrusted to us; all the opportunities we have to grow in wisdom, in grace and in love; all the ways we have to apply what we have learned; and all the days we have to live our faith and to remain faithful, are from Jesus and for Jesus.

What we do with all this and what becomes of it depends, in part, on who we rely upon for truth and guidance, who we follow, and who we glorify above all. Until we recognize, receive, follow, and give thanks to the Source of it all we are unlikely to know the Spirit, the Promise and the Purpose of it all. If this understanding is missing from what we are doing, then what we are doing is missing the most important understanding.

Christ Jesus said "*I am with you always*."

We are not alone, no matter how far we are from loved ones; no matter how far we are from safety; no matter how far we are from compassion and support; no matter how isolated, broken hearted or afraid we are; we are never forgotten and we are never alone.

Jesus said, *"Behold, I have graven you on the palms of my hands; your walls are continually before me"* (Isaiah 49:16). If we, in the frailty of our humanity and the activities that occupy our lives can remember the people we love and serve and suffer for, it should come as no surprise that the Lord not only knows us, every one of us, but He never forgets us—never.

The amazing love our Savior has for us is a part of our spirit, as well. Those we love are imprinted on our hearts forever. We see them clearly even when we are absent from them, and love them forever even when they are far from us.

Such love is a reflection of its origin. Our lives bear the fruit of such love because we are connected to the source of such love. Apart from it we cannot comprehend it, nor bear the fruit that reflects it.

Trees

The trees in our midst are a beautiful reminder of this connection. The fruit of a tree does not give rise to the root; rather, the fruit is a reflection of its vital connection with the steadfastness, strength, support and provisions of the root. The genetic code of the root is imprinted in the seeds of the fruit. When the seeds are sown and a seedling grows, its root gives rise to it and supports it, just as it did for the tree from which it came.

In like manner, the Lord told King David to tell his son Solomon to *"Arise and be doing! The Lord be with you!"* (1 Chronicles 22:16).

Our Maker, Sustainer, Redeemer and Lord wanted Solomon to know that the root of his great grandfather Obed (Ruth 4:17), his grandfather Jesse (Romans 15:12), his father David and the root of Solomon were one in the same. The Lord preceded and gave life to each of them and blessed and supported them. His promise was to be with Solomon, too, just as He was with our mom and dad and our grandparents before us and as He is with each of us and our children and our children's children. He is our source, our supply, our root—our Lord, Christ Jesus.

Trees are a beautiful and daily reminder of this reality. Trees depend on their roots. Their strength and stability rise from their roots. Their blessings to us (which span generations) are intimately connected to their roots. Their fruit reflects the unseen provisions of their roots. The trees' roots support life and are the foundation from which the benefits they yield each day reach wider, higher and further throughout their lives. Apart from their roots, trees suffer and fall.

Our foundation, the Lord Jesus, does the same for us and much more. It is in His love we live. It is by His Spirit we grow. It is through His provisions we bear fruit. It is with His support we reach out. It is upon His life and promise we depend and are born again.

We may choose not to believe that Christ Jesus is with us. We may choose not to believe He is our source and our supply. We may choose not to honor Him. We may even choose not to be a part of Him. He does not overrule our free will. He will weep for us because He knows that apart from Him, His "trees" suffer and fall. An example of this is recorded in the book of Numbers.

God delivered His people from bondage in Egypt. He was with them and provided for their daily needs; yet, their murmurings, contention and rebellion against Him and against His servants Moses and Aaron (who He appointed to care for them and their history), filled their lives and fulfilled their fear they would perish in the desert.

None of those, twenty years of age and older, ever made their home in the land God had promised them and "their children suffered for their faithlessness" (see Numbers 14:33). It is one thing for us to suffer for the choices we make. It is much worse when we subject our children to suffering for the choices we make.

Our answer to the question, *"Do you love me more than these?"* extends beyond our lifetimes. Our answer ripples through time and eternity in the lives of our children and our children's children; in the lives of people we were blessed to meet and serve; and in everything entrusted to our care for the glory of Christ, for serving one another and for what we leave behind. It follows us wherever we go.

Our answer reflects more than a momentary pause in our busy lives to consider our love for Christ Jesus. It is the choice that inspires every other choice we make. We have seen this, for we have lived it with members of our family and closest friends, each of whom are imprinted on our hearts, inspiring and influencing our choices.

Affirmation of this is our daily thought of them, our faithfulness and thankfulness for them, and the evidence in our lives in the way we treat one another. Their spirit is at work in and through us. Our spirit reflects the spirit of the one to whom our heart belongs.

We may not always reflect them, but we are always connected to them even when we are not always like them. We love them even when our choices do not reflect or serve them, and we do not keep them first in our thoughts.

Perhaps we focus more on what we want, what we think, what we are doing, and on what others think and are doing than on what Jesus thinks, wants and is doing. If our response to this is, "We have no way of knowing what Jesus thinks, or is doing or what He wants," then one of a few things may be happening. (1) We are not following Jesus very closely. (2) We are not spending much time in His Word. (3) We are not thinking about and applying to our lives what He said and what He did. (4) We are drifting away from Him.

We may drift away from Him even if we are convinced this could not possibly be happening to us. Like a boat carried along by the tide and the winds, we may drift far from our foundation, losing both our direction and our destination. Searching the horizon, it may look much the same. There seems to be no apparent change or consequence caused by the drift. If we do not recognize we are drifting, we will not see how far we have drifted.

We can recognize this by the way we interact with one another:

- justifying our behavior, words and choices no matter how unkind, destructive or ungodly they may be;
- by the motives and means of those we support, follow and believe;
- by gratitude and honor we give to men, women and families who have served, protected and sacrificed for our country;
- by our focus, faithfulness and stewardship of everything our great God has given us to protect and to lift up for His glory;
- by whether we trust God is sovereign and that He will accomplish all His purpose;
- by the spirit we have for our Savior's suffering and resurrection;
- by keeping Jesus' promise within us. *"I will not leave you desolate: I will come to you"* (John 14:18).

Jesus is with us. We are graven into His hands. He provides for all our needs. *"For the Lord your God has blessed you in all the work of your hands; He knows your going through this great wilderness; these forty years the Lord your God has been with you; you have lacked nothing"* (Deuteronomy 2:7).

Jesus is interceding for us (see Romans 8:34). Jesus is preparing a place for us (see John 14:3). We are in His prayers (see John 17:20). We are in His providential care. We are on His mind. He is making ready a homecoming for us. What a blessing to know when we are adrift — even when we seem to be isolated and are afraid; even when we are sure we have failed Him and are forgotten; and even when we do not understand the adversity or affliction in our lives—we are not alone. The Creator of Heaven and earth is with us.

So the question, *"Do you love me more than these?"* brings our hearts and minds to bear on how much we love Jesus.

What it may not bring to mind as often is how much the Lord Jesus truly loves us. No matter how we profess to love and follow Him, if we do not know how much He loves us; if we do not trust He is with us; if we do not acknowledge who He is, if we do not *"bless Him for the good land He has given us"* and protect it (Deuteronomy 8:10); if we do not intentionally and confidently yield to His Spirit in us and let Him inspire and lead us; if what we say and do does not honor Him and it is not our fervent prayer that it does; if we are too busy to remember Him and to thank Him; if we identify ourselves, our power and determination as the source and reason for all that is in our care (see Deuteronomy 8:17); then we have overlooked, forgotten, or never fully cherished the greatness of the love and purpose Jesus has for each one of us.

If we do cherish His love and walk in it each day, our reply will be like Simon Peter's, *"Lord, you know everything; you know that I love you"* (John 21:17). Our answer will express the source and the power and the person who loved us first, who loves us most and who loves us forever.

What if we have never experienced that love? What if we know nothing about the love of Jesus personally? In that case, either the Son of God — the King of kings, the Lord of lords, sovereign, holy, almighty, who suffered in our place to give us eternal life, who promised He would always be with us — has forsaken us and left us alone, or we have forsaken Him and chosen to walk alone.

We may not believe or recognize the countless times Jesus has lifted us up, comforted us, protected us, supported us, inspired us, informed us, trusted us, warned us, tested us, rescued us, disciplined us, humbled us, healed us, restored us, equipped us, enabled us, encouraged us, sheltered us, fed us, guided us, strengthened us, chosen us, called us, sent us, went before us, heard us, answered us, blessed us and held us close to His heart.

Whether we understand how much He loves us or not, it does not change how much He loves us. Whether we know He is with us or not, it does not change His presence with us. Whether we know He is the source of every blessing in our life or not, it does not change Him from being the source of every blessing in our lives. The change that comes from knowing His love does not change Jesus—it changes each of us, individually.

For The Love of Jesus

Before we had knowledge of His love, the phrase "for the love of Jesus" may have had many different applications in our lives. Perhaps we said it in a burst of anger, frustration or disrespect. Maybe we said it or thought it in a moment of humility, gratitude and reverence. Perhaps we prayed it so that our choices, words and deeds might serve Jesus. Regardless, each one misses something that we must not miss.

If, when we think of the phrase "for the love of Jesus", or use it, we consider it only from our point of view, we have missed the Lord's point of view. We have missed seeing with His eyes; forgiving and loving with His Spirit; protecting and lifting up all that is from Him: our faith, our loved ones, our country, one another, our work, our thoughts, our hearts, the words we speak, the times, places, resources and opportunities we have, the choices we make, the great price He paid for all; the great love He has for all.

If we do not know, in a personal way, His love — if we do not know His prayers for us, what He has done for us, what He is doing for us and all He is preparing for us; if we do not know He is with us and is faithful to us even when we are not faithful to Him — if we do not know these things, then we do not know Jesus. To say, "Yes, Lord, I love you" and mean it, we must know Jesus and receive His love; believe His love; apply His love; share His love; and treasure His love. There is nothing in all of time and space like His love and there is no one who loves us like Jesus.

To love Jesus more does not require us to love one another less; quite the opposite. Our love for one another, our country, and for every blessing in our care is not diminished by loving Jesus more. Rather, loving Jesus more will produce greater care, greater protection, greater devotion and greater effectiveness for all we love because our love is rooted in and inspired by Him. Our love for Jesus and His love within us expands our love for all. Perhaps, then, we may pray a prayer like this:

> *Holy Father, Your Word says Your Name is blessed in all nations and in all the earth. Your Word says, "bless the Lord oh my soul and all that is within me." Your Word says You loved the world so much You gave Your only Son that whoever believes in Him shall not perish but have eternal life. Your Word says to love one another as You have loved us. Your Word says to know the love of Christ that we may be filled with all the fullness of God. Your Word says You will be with us always. Oh God, thank You for Your Word. Help us to remember and to obey Your Word, and to know the love of Jesus, and to live to love Jesus more. Amen.*

In Our Conversations

Can we love Jesus more, yet never mention His name? Can we see the beauty Jesus has created in the earth, sky and sea, and not praise His name? Can we receive countless blessings from Jesus, and not rejoice in His name? Can we serve Jesus, the giver and restorer of life, and not glorify His name? Can we remember to honor, adore and share His great name with someone in our conversations today?

Christ Jesus knows whether we will, as He knew whether Simon Peter would, and the Lord of life asks so we may know: *"Do you love me more than these?"*

Epilogue

The day is approaching when we will know far more than we do now, no matter how capable, accomplished or resourceful we are. We may even learn how little we know about what matters most and how little love we gave to the one who matters most.

What we see and hear may not be what we expect. It may be what we failed to see and to hear, though it was always near.

We may find that what we missed was the result of our own choices. Should that be so, we may instinctively claim some cause beyond our control and understanding. Seeking vindication, we may refuse to believe or admit that the cause was not someone or something outside ourselves, but it was always inside of us.

We may explain it and justify, but our choices are motivated and determined by what our heart wants, not by what our Lord wants. Asking for God's Word, His permission and waiting for His timing may not have been in our thoughts.

The significance and the irony of this cannot be overlooked. We often seek council and wisdom from someone we are close to (someone we trust) before making a decision. It may be a loved one, a friend or someone we identify with or even follow on social media; but they are not the reason we do what we do—our heart is the reason.

If our heart longs to know Jesus better, to follow Jesus closer, and to love Jesus more, then by the power of the Holy Spirit in us, we will.

What a blessing to hear Jesus say: *"Truly, I say to you, many prophets and righteous men longed to see what you see, and did not see it, and to hear what you hear, and did not hear it"* (Matthew 13:17).

By the power of the Spirit of God, we remember Jesus in breaking the bread and drinking the cup; we serve Jesus with all He entrusts into our care; we honor Jesus through our choices and our prayers; and we understand and confess, "Oh, Lord, I should have loved You more!"

Trees and Love for Jesus

From their beginning, trees grow.
Love for Jesus grows, too.

A slender stem and root holds fast to its place.
Embryonic leaves unfold, reaching for the light.
By God's grace and providence, the little tree grows.

Weeks become seasons.
Cold nights, dry days, storms and whirlwinds come and go.
Through it all the young tree grows, blessed by the light.
Now it faces challenges it never knew until it grew.

Seasons become years.
The tree reaches higher and wider, receiving the light.
Inside its mature frame is the tiny tree from which it came.
With growth, the tree produces more of the blessings God created it for.

From their beginning, trees grow.
Love for Jesus grows, too.

CPSIA information can be obtained
at www.ICGtesting.com
Printed in the USA
BVHW091755021121
620556BV00016B/361

9 781662 829475